MODERN
CLASSIC
COCKTAILS

MODERN
CLASSIC
COCKTAILS

60+ Stories and Recipes from the New Golden Age in Drinks

ROBERT SIMONSON

Photos by Lizzie Munro

TEN SPEED PRESS
California | New York

TO MARY KATE MURRAY,
MY WIFE, COUNSELOR, SOULMATE, AND LOVE

CONTENTS

MODERN CLASSICS

MODERN CLASSICS TO BE

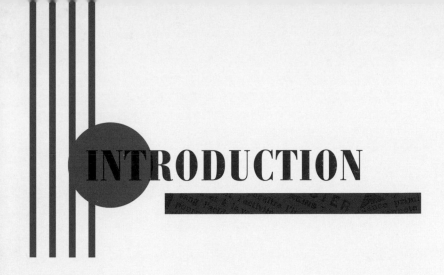

INTRODUCTION

The greatest dividend of the cocktail revival of the early twenty-first century has been the relentless creativity of its participating bartenders. More new cocktails—and *good* ones—have been invented in the past thirty years than during any period since the first golden age of cocktails, which lasted from the 1870s until the arrival of Prohibition in 1920.

That initial bar-world zenith produced dozens of classic recipes—drinks we still enjoy today—like the Martini, Martinez, Manhattan, Rob Roy, Daiquiri, Clover Club, Tom Collins, Sazerac, Jack Rose, and many, many more. This century's eruption of talent has handily delivered its own trove of drinks that are likely to endure.

But what actually makes a new cocktail a modern classic?

It is a question I've devoted a lot of thought to over recent years (and an entire cocktail app, "Modern Classics of the Cocktail Renaissance," created with Martin Doudoroff). Calling a drink that was invented five, ten, or even twenty years ago a "classic" can sound like a bit of a stretch. It's doubtful anyone in 1899 was already calling the Manhattan a classic cocktail, or even thought about drinks in such terms. But the cocktail renaissance has moved along at breakneck speed. So much progress was crammed into the aughts that each year of that decade felt more like dog years. And those achievements spread like wildfire, thanks to the advent of the internet, which coincided almost exactly with the rise of cocktail culture and opened up multiple avenues of information among bartenders, as well as between bartenders and the media and cocktail enthusiasts. Within the framework of this hive of activity it was possible for a new drink like the Oaxaca Old-Fashioned—an early cocktail using mezcal, invented by Phil Ward at Death & Co. in New York—to be created in 2007 and become recognized as a benchmark achievement by 2010.

The Oaxaca Old-Fashioned embodies one characteristic any modern classic cocktail must have: it traveled beyond the bar where it was created. It is possible, surely, for a drink to become famous and still be served only at its place of origin. The Dukes Martini, for example, is known the world over for its arctic-cold, undiluted presentation and its use of only a few dashes of vermouth, but very few bars serve a Martini the peculiar way the Dukes Bar in London does. That makes it not a modern classic, but a house specialty.

The Oaxaca Old-Fashioned, on the other hand, was not only a common order at Death & Co. but within a year or two of its debut was being served at numerous bars around the world. A drink's adoption by dozens of additional bars is a certain signifier that a cocktail is on its way to attaining classic status. (Sometimes this particular drink—a simple Old-Fashioned riff made with reposado tequila and mezcal—is sold under a different name, but it is the same cocktail nevertheless.)

No drink lands on a competing bar's menu if the new bar's owner and the bartenders don't approve of it. Therein lies a second tip-off that a drink has made the grade: brothers and sisters in armbands like it, drink it, and freely acknowledge that one of their colleagues has cooked up something unusually good. There is great camaraderie among members of the bartending community, but compliments about new drinks aren't doled out unless they're meant. Putting a colleague's cocktail on their menu is the ultimate affirmation. The Old Cuban—Audrey Saunders's rum-and-Champagne-based Mojito spin, created in New York—quickly crossed the Atlantic and was served at bars in London and Paris within a decade of its birth. Few of those bar owners had ever met Saunders, but they knew a good drink when they tasted one.

There are other indicators. When a drink inspires variations on its original formula, that's another sure tell that a cocktail deserves the title modern classic. The recipe for the Red Hook, Vincenzo Errico's riff on the Brooklyn cocktail, has spawned dozens of additional drinks, all in the Manhattan or Brooklyn cocktail family. Similarly, the Penicillin—a mix of blended scotch, lemon juice, ginger syrup, and smoky single-malt Scotch created by Sam Ross at Milk & Honey in 2005—has served as inspiration for dozens of other drinks around the world. In Ross's native Australia, for example, a Sydney bar called the Lobo Plantation offered a Penicilina, a tequila version of the drink. Ross himself has riffed on his own cocktail, creating frozen and hot versions. (Sometimes a riff on a modern classic can result in yet another modern classic. Sam Ross's popular Paper Plane—made of bourbon, amaro, Aperol, and lemon juice—inspired Joaquín Simó's Naked & Famous, made of mezcal, yellow Chartreuse, Aperol, and lime juice.)

The final litmus test of a modern classic cocktail is that it must, of course, be popular. It can't just be admired by critics and bar-industry types. People have to order it, and not just during its initial heyday, but for years afterward. The Espresso Martini (originally called—and listed in this book as—the Vodka Espresso) and Cosmopolitan, for example, were invented in the 1980s, and we still drink them today. The same goes for the Tommy's Margarita, invented in the 1990s, and the Porn Star Martini, which today is among the most popular cocktails in the United Kingdom, nearly two decades after it was created in London by Douglas Ankrah. You can't fake that kind of track record.

There is, perhaps, one additional and amusing clue that a drink has surely become a classic: historical confusion. Many bartenders have told me anecdotal stories about customers—and even fellow bartenders—who have insisted that the Gold Rush, Penicillin, Revolver, and other modern cocktails included in this book are of pre-Prohibition vintage. As such myths take hold, a bartender can find themself in the bewildering position of being unable to convince customers that they actually invented the famous cocktail the drinker is holding in their hand. When everyone thinks your drink is an old standby, one created way back when by someone long dead, you know your drink has arrived.

The more than sixty drinks that follow all earned their stripes as modern classics years ago. Sprinkled among them are a handful of critic's choices—potential classics that I feel have the goods to become popular go-to cocktails in the future. They are signified by the Modern Classic to Be label.

You may notice that the bulk of the drinks in this book come from a specific and rather narrow time frame, roughly 2007 to 2012. Within that span, 2008 and 2009 are particularly well represented. Those were fecund years that produced an embarrassment of liquid riches destined for the ages. In fact, I would argue that 2009 was the very apex of the cocktail revival—what 1925 was for literature, 1939 was for Hollywood, and 1969 was for rock music.

It was during this stretch of years that a perfect storm of circumstances came together, leading to peak bartender ingenuity. Among them: a dedicated community of passionate mixologists determined to bring their profession back to prominence and claim a seat at the culinary table; the opening of a group of pioneering bars devoted specifically to the craft of the cocktail; the return to the market of dozens of forgotten or neglected spirits that were critical to filling out the mixologist's arsenal of flavors; renewed access to a once-lost library of

out-of-print bar manuals and recipe books, brought back to light by a handful of collectors and enthusiasts; and a professional blank slate, created by four decades of industry neglect—a fresh start that allowed for the creation of drinks that were both simple yet excitingly new.

But all storms subside. No revival can go on forever. I would locate the curtain call of the modern cocktail renaissance roughly in 2017. That same year, food writer Kevin Alexander, writing in Thrillist—and drawing heavily on *A Proper Drink*, a history of the cocktail renaissance that I had published the previous year—declared loudly, "The Craft Cocktail Revolution Is Over. Now What?" Alexander's point was that the war for mixed-drink legitimacy had been won. Great cocktails were back to stay. It was no longer headline-grabbing news that bartending wizards spun out great cocktails, but simply laudable quotidian work. Every new restaurant or bar, of whatever type, had a beverage director and a cocktail menu. The media stopped breathlessly writing up every brash new cocktail place that opened. Quality mixed drinks were expected. They were also expected by the public. Today's consumers came of age when the cocktail revival was in high gear, or after it had already happened and settled in. It was part of their world as they were growing up. Young drinkers are relatively unfazed by the perfectly balanced, beautifully presented, and lovingly garnished libation the bartender has just set on the branded coaster before them. To them, it has always been thus.

At the same time, the cocktail community that was forged so suddenly and so forcefully in the aughts began to splinter in the late 2010s. Bartending pioneers got older. They started families and settled down. Some retired or left the industry. Others moved into the punch-the-clock stability of corporate work, often as brand ambassadors for liquor conglomerates. Still other bartenders started up cocktail consultancy firms. A few went into distilling, launching their own liquor brands or canned and bottled cocktails. And a too-large number of leaders died tragically young, including Douglas Ankrah, Henry Besant, Rob Cooper, John Lermayer, Sasha Petraske, and Dick Bradsell. Petraske, who founded Milk & Honey—the most influential cocktail bar of the past quarter century—in New York, and Bradsell, the godfather of the London cocktail scene, were largely responsible for the cocktail revivals in the United States and United Kingdom, respectively. Once they were gone, their shoes were never truly filled.

Other leaders of the movement eventually took a step back, realizing that the rock-and-roll lifestyle that goes along with bar work cannot be maintained indefinitely. This trend—one that was shared by many cocktail lovers on the other side of the bar—led in part to the advancement in the late 2010s of drinks that were lighter and lower in alcohol content. Highballs and spritzes enjoyed a new heyday. That trend eventually led to no-ABV (alcohol by volume) "cock-tails," previously called mocktails but now bearing more sophisticated names and more complex makeups. Prominent cocktail figures who once hawked the biggest and booziest of drinks now sang the praises of nonalcoholic "spirits."

The cocktail community has faced other social challenges as well, ones that go beyond the obvious dangers represented by their central product. The social upheavals of the MeToo and Black Lives Matter movements exposed the bar world as being as guilty as any industry of sexism, inequality, and a lack of diversity and inclusivity. And environmental issues got bars thinking about the ultimate sustainability of their businesses, which do not have a tiny carbon foot-print. Then came the Covid-19 pandemic—the ultimate erasure of achievement. It took down Milk & Honey in London, Pegu Club and Existing Conditions in New York, Marvel Bar in Minneapolis, Bar Agricole in San Francisco, Sauvage and Donna in Brooklyn, Eastern Standard and The Hawthorne in Boston, and dozens of other important bars. Many bars that had been inspired by those giants sur-vive as of this writing, so the legacy remains, but the originals are gone.

But then, every revolution eventually repeats itself. Back in the late nine-teenth century, during the first golden age of the cocktail, bartenders and drinkers probably thought great cocktails would flow on year after year, world without end. No such thing happened. Prohibition saw to that. And today, the accomplishments of the late twentieth and early twenty-first centuries are sometimes forgotten—or not known at all—by fresh generations of bartenders and drinkers. In the summer of 2021, the New York press excitedly announced in separate articles that the Cosmopolitan and the Espresso Martini—two of the foundational pillars of the early cocktail revival, which became totems of the 1990s—were *back*. Veterans of the revival raised a graying eyebrow and won-dered, *Were they ever gone?*

In the face of such cyclical forgetfulness, it is important to set down for the record the achievements of the recent past. When the cocktail revival began, there were nothing but questions. Who had created what drinks? Where and when were they invented? How were the cocktails best made? What were the proper techniques? What were the correct spirits? How do you even make a proper Martini or Manhattan or Old-Fashioned? *How do we do any of this?*

We only knew that the cocktail was an American invention that was once held in very high esteem throughout the world. But finding the evidence to back up that boast was difficult. All the relevant books that might have explained it were out of print; the newspaper articles that chronicled the lives of bars and bartenders were buried in the library somewhere. And so the digging began. Recipe by recipe, bar by bar, mixologist by mixologist, the history of the

cocktail was reassembled, with many missteps and misconceptions along the way. It got done, but it was slow, arduous work.

This book, like *A Proper Drink* before it, exists so that we don't have to go through all that again. The internet that helped the cocktail revival blossom is now the enemy, a jumble of misinformation and inaccuracies about the history of modern drinks. Most of the very recipes for the cocktails are wrong. There's no reason this should be so. The cocktail revival is still fairly recent, its history fresh and excavatable, many of its major players still active. All that's needed is to gather the facts and compile them. Even now, that's a tricky task, as history created in a bar is always going to be history as seen through a smudged rocks glass, and some of the memories of bartenders can resemble the jottings on a stained, crumpled bar napkin trapped under the leg of a bar stool. But we've taken on the challenge of writing it all down, so that the tipplers of the next era or two don't have trouble figuring out how to properly build a Chartreuse Swizzle. That is what this book aims to accomplish. Cheers!

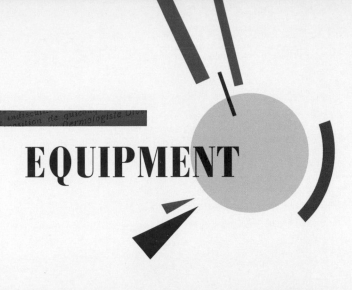

EQUIPMENT

I would recommend investing in each of the items listed here. Presentation and precision go a long way toward making a good cocktail. If you shop wisely, it needn't cost you much—maybe fifty dollars, tops. And the outlay will pay dividends for years to come.

GLASSWARE. The various drinks that follow call for a cocktail or a coupe glass (5 to 6 ounces), an old-fashioned or rocks glass (4 to 10 ounces), or a collins glass (10 to 14 ounces). Always keep your glasses chilled for at least 15 minutes, and do not remove them from the freezer until ready to use. If you forgot to pre-chill the glasses, a quick fix is to fill the glasses with ice and let them chill while you prepare the cocktails.

STANDARD MIXING GLASS. A pint glass can do in a pinch if you don't have a dedicated mixing glass. I prefer mixing glasses to cocktail tins, because you can see through glass and keep track of how much you are diluting your drink. Many barware companies sell beautiful cut-glass mixing glasses. Naturally, these are more expensive than a standard pint glass, but they are a beautiful addition to any home bar and add elegance to the drink-building ritual.

BOSTON SHAKER. This two-piece shaker, composed of a standard mixing glass and a metal mixing tin, is suitable for both stirred drinks (for which you need only the mixing glass) and shaken drinks (for which you require both parts).

BARSPOON. A long barspoon (approximately 11 inches) is the preferred tool for stirring drinks.

JIGGER. Most jiggers have a dual-measure design. Typically, they measure either 1 ounce on one end and ½ ounce on the other, or 1½ ounces and ¾ ounce. Modern Mixologist makes a very versatile double jigger: one end has a 1½-ounce capacity, the other a 1-ounce capacity.

COCKTAIL STRAINER. Julep strainers, which have a perforated bowl, are for drinks made solely of spirits. However, a hawthorne strainer, which is lined with a coiled spring for catching citrus pulp, will do the job as well.

MUDDLER. A muddler is required for certain drinks that ask you to mash up fruits, vegetables, herbs, or sugar cubes at the bottom of a mixing glass or serving glass. Old-fashioned wooden models work best.

TRAYS OR MOLDS FOR LARGE ICE CUBES. A large ice cube makes a big difference, both aesthetically and tastewise, in some stirred sipping drinks, such as variations on the Old-Fashioned and Negroni. Molds for these sorts of cubes, typically 1½ or 2 inches, are now widely available, both online and in stores.

If you want to get particular and don't mind spending a little extra, I recommend the bar equipment put out by Cocktail Kingdom (www.cocktailkingdom .com) and Modern Mixologist (www.themodernmixologist.com). Full disclosure: Cocktail Kingdom and I have collaborated on a set of old-fashioned glasses. If you want to have a little fun shopping, antique and vintage shops, as well as yard sales and garage sales, are good sources for old cocktail glasses and coupes of various designs and styles.

INGREDIENTS

The cocktail renaissance has spurred an increase in the production and availability of quality spirits, liqueurs, and bitters. In most cities now there are at least one or two well-curated liquor shops that can satisfy a home mixologist's every spirituous need.

ICE. I cannot overemphasize the importance of using good ice when mixing these drinks. Keep your ice fresh. If ice has been sitting in your freezer for more than a couple of days, do not use it in a drink. Throw it out and make a fresh batch. Old ice has absorbed other flavors lurking in your freezer. Also, if your local tap water is not of sterling quality, I recommend using filtered or bottled water for your ice.

When making any of these drinks, do not be stingy with the ice. Fill your mixing glass nearly to the rim. Cocktails should be as cold as possible.

BITTERS. A dash is whatever comes out of a bottle of bitters when you upend it with a swift flick of the wrist. Be careful, though; some bitters bottles dispense more quickly than others. Angostura aromatic bitters is the most famous brand and a product you must have in your arsenal. Second most important are orange bitters. In the past decade, the market has become flooded with orange bitters. Regans' No. 6 is the most common. Some combine Regans' with Fee Brothers to create a more well-rounded orange bitters (referred to as Feegan's). Angostura orange bitters is another prominent brand. The third most important bitters you'll need is Peychaud's. And one drink herein calls for peach bitters.

GARNISHES. Just as much as bitters, garnishes form a vital part of the cocktail. If you don't have the called-for lemons, oranges, limes, grapefruits, or cocktail cherries on hand, don't make the drink.

Be sure your citrus fruits are fresh and firm, with plenty of skin from which to carve your twists. Wash all fruits before using them; they may be covered with residual pesticides and other chemicals. To make a twist, use a vegetable peeler (a simple Y-shaped peeler will do) and try to cut away just the zest, leaving behind as much of the bitter white pith as possible. Express, or twist, the garnish over the surface of the drink to release the citrus oils, and then slip it into the drink or hang it over the rim of the glass. Don't rub the twist along the rim, as it can leave a bitter taste that will inform every sip.

I recommend making cocktail cherries from scratch rather than buying a jar at the store. There are many recipes for brandied cherries to be found on the internet. It is worth the effort and will greatly improve your drinks. Use sour cherries, which have a short season during the summer, not the ubiquitous sweet variety.

STIRRING AND SHAKING. "Stir until chilled" usually means stirring for about 15 to 30 seconds. Where shaking is called for, shake vigorously for 10 to 15 seconds.

SIMPLE SYRUP. In many of the following recipes, simple syrup is called for. It is a mix of sugar and water, gently cooked at a low heat until the sugar is dissolved and then allowed to cool. Where the recipe lists no ratio of sugar to water, use one part sugar to one part water. Where the recipe says "(2:1)," the ratio is two parts sugar to one part water. The same formula applies to the honey syrups listed in this book. For other syrups, special recipes are provided.

MODERN CLASSIC COCKTAILS

RECIPES AND STORIES

AMARETTO SOUR

Jeffrey Morgenthaler, a bartender who worked at Clyde Common in Portland, Oregon, for many years, is the shepherd of unloved drinks. "There are no bad drinks, only bad bartenders," he has said, and he means it. As good as his word, he has devoted his labors to rescuing déclassé drinks like the Grasshopper, Blue Hawaii, and Long Island Iced Tea. But his most successful salvage job has been the Amaretto Sour.

"I always liked Amaretto Sours," he said. "I drank them in college sometimes. Then, when everyone started getting super serious about drinks, it just kinda got left by the wayside. I remember seeing other bartenders talk about the 'dark days' of cocktails, and they'd always mention the Amaretto Sour as an example of how terrible the drinks were back in the day." So, around 2009, he went about improving it. His chief innovation—and the one that took the drink from tacky to terrific—was the addition of nearly an ounce of quality overproof bourbon.

He put the recipe on his popular blog around 2012. By 2014, he bravely put it on the menu at Clyde Common. But it was at Pépé le Moko, a kitschy subterranean bar that opened beneath Clyde Common in 2014, that the cocktail became a star.

"It was probably our number one seller along with the Grasshopper," he recalled. "People seemed kinda relieved that they could go to a fancy cocktail bar and have fun drinks for once." The drink has since become the default recipe for the Amaretto Sour at craft cocktail bars around the world.

1½ ounces amaretto
¾ ounce bourbon, preferably Booker's
1 ounce lemon juice
1 teaspoon simple syrup (2:1)
½ ounce egg white, beaten
Lemon twist for garnish
Brandied cherry for garnish

Dry shake all the ingredients except the garnishes—that is, shake them up without ice—in a cocktail shaker. Add ice to the shaker and shake again, about 15 seconds. Strain into a rocks glass filled with ice. Garnish with a lemon twist and brandied cherry.

ANCIENT MARINER

The Ancient Mariner is tiki evangelist Jeff "Beachbum" Berry's early effort to re-create the Navy Grog, his favorite cocktail by tiki icon Victor Bergeron, aka "Trader Vic." The task was not an easy one. In the 1990s, when Berry began his journey of discovery, the tiki world of Los Angeles was a diaspora of bartenders who held, but would not share, the recipes to the bygone cocktail glories of Trader Vic and his tiki archrival, Donn Beach of Don the Beachcomber. Published recipes were all but nonexistent, as tiki bartending had always been a proprietary, secretive art. (The super-unhelpful recipe for the Navy Grog published in a sales pamphlet called only for "Trader Vic Navy Grog Rum" and "Trader Vic Navy Grog Mix"—two extinct products.) Berry resorted to guesswork and reverse-engineering to create his version of the drink. A crucial key to unlocking the recipe came when fellow L.A. cocktail nerd Ted Haigh uncovered a stash of bottles of the discontinued Wray & Nephew Pimento Dram at a liquor store in Costa Mesa called Hi-Time Wine Cellars. Tasting it for the first time was an "aha!" moment for Berry; pimento (aka Jamaican allspice) was the secret flavoring used in Vic's Navy Grog mix. Two veteran tiki bartenders, Tony Ramos at Madame Wu's and Mike Buhen at the Tiki-Ti, confirmed Berry's hunch.

Further tinkering got Berry to the recipe offered here, which is not strictly a Trader Vic Navy Grog, but his interpretation of it. Stripped away were honey and the white rum. The entire process took years. "I called it the Ancient Mariner partly because by the time I finished with it, that's how old I felt," Berry said.

The drink first appeared in 1994 in Berry's DIY version of the Grog Log, a xeroxed, folded, and stapled zine-like recipe collection that he gave away for free. The Log was given a proper publication in 1998. A decade later, the drink made its first appearance on a cocktail menu at Rivera in downtown L. A. It has since also been sold at bars in New York, Boston, New Orleans, Athens, and Melbourne, and published in volumes like the Mr. Boston bartending guide. It even has its own Wikipedia page.

1 ounce Demerara rum, preferably El Dorado 8-year or Hamilton 86 Demerara River rum

1 ounce dark Jamaican rum, preferably Coruba Original Blend rum, Appleton Estate Rare Blend aged 12 years rum, or Myers's Original Dark rum

¾ ounce lime juice

½ ounce white grapefruit juice

½ ounce simple syrup

¼ ounce pimento dram

Mint sprig for garnish

Lime wedge for garnish

Combine all ingredients except the garnishes in a cocktail shaker half-filled with ice. Shake until chilled, about 15 seconds. Strain into a double old-fashioned glass filled with crushed ice. Garnish with a mint sprig and lime wedge.

ART OF CHOKE

The Violet Hour, one of the first important craft cocktail bars in Chicago, produced a number of sleeper hits during its first couple of years in business, including this fluke from bartender Kyle Davidson. One night, Davidson fielded a "bartender's choice" order (that is, a drink bartenders serve to patrons who give them free rein) from a customer asking for rum and bitters. He whipped together a mix of white rum and Cynar, gave the glass a green Chartreuse rinse and a mint-leaf garnish, and sent it out. When he was later called on to create an amaro drink for the menu, Davidson refined the drink, increasing the percentage of Cynar and Chartreuse, relegating the rum to spiritous scaffolding, and upping the mint's role through muddling. Most audaciously, he added lime juice but kept the cocktail a stirred drink. (Drinks with juice are typically shaken.)

The Art of Choke was a local industry secret for a while. But Davidson took the drink to every bar he worked at, including the popular Chicago restaurant the Publican, where it was batched and offered to diners as a shot called "Kyle's After Pork" digestif. With that, and its inclusion in the influential 2009 book *Rogue Cocktails* as well as its sequel *Beta Cocktails*, news of the drink got around to the right people—that is, other bartenders. It was also featured in Brad Thomas Parsons's widely read book *Amaro*.

---

1 ounce light rum	Muddle one of the mint sprigs
1 ounce Cynar	with the liquid ingredients in a
¾ teaspoon lime juice	mixing glass. Add ice and stir
¾ teaspoon rich	until chilled, about 15 seconds.
Demerara syrup (2:1)	Strain into a rocks glass filled
¼ ounce green Chartreuse	with ice. Garnish with the
2 mint sprigs	remaining mint sprig.

BASIL GIMLET

This herbal sour was a sensation in San Francisco in the mid-aughts. Greg Lindgren owned Rye, one of the first important craft cocktail bars in the city. His wife, Shelley Lindgren, was a noted sommelier. One day in 2005, Shelley was traveling for work in Boston, where she encountered a vodka gimlet with muddled basil at the restaurant Via Matta. She passed the idea on to Greg, who adopted the idea for the just-opened Rye. Greg substituted gin for vodka and called it a Basil Gimlet. (Via Matta had called it, somewhat redundantly, a Basil-Lime Gimlet.) The rest was history.

2 ounces gin, preferably Junipero
1 ounce lime juice
½ ounce simple syrup
6 fresh basil leaves

Muddle 5 of the basil leaves with the simple syrup at bottom of a cocktail shaker. Add the gin and lime juice. Shake until chilled, about 15 seconds. Fine strain into a chilled coupe. Garnish with the remaining basil leaf.

BENTON'S OLD-FASHIONED

There is perhaps no stronger tie between a drink and a bar than that between the Benton's Old-Fashioned and PDT. This bacon fat–washed version of the classic was a sensation from the day it was put on the menu at the East Village speakeasy in 2007. Bartender Don Lee created it using Benton's bacon fat, borrowed from chef David Chang's nearby restaurant Momofuku.

"Looking at American whiskey and the other food traditions of that area, smoked meats [were] a part of that," said Lee. "The first spirit I tried to make the Benton's Old-Fashioned with was George Dickel whiskey, because Benton's comes from Tennessee, so I wanted to use a Tennessee whiskey." At that time, it was impossible to get hold of Dickel, so Lee ended up switching to the Four Roses Yellow Label bourbon.

Lee didn't invent the fat-washing technique for cocktails; other bartenders, like Eben Freeman, had experimented with it before him. But the Benton's Old-Fashioned popularized the approach.

PDT took the drink off the menu soon after its initial appearance. That didn't go over well. "In the weeks and months after we took the Benton's Old-Fashioned off the menu, many guests who had either tried it when we served it, read about it, or heard about it from a friend, requested it," recalled Jim Meehan, who ran the bar at the time. "It became tiresome and counterintuitive not to bring it back." Benton's has been PDT's best-selling drink ever since; the bar sells roughly 150 a week, according to owner Jeff Bell. It's also, incidentally, the top seller at PDT Hong Kong.

"If you had to pick one drink that defines PDT's approach and legacy under my watch, I'd say it would be the Benton's Old-Fashioned," says Meehan.

---

2 ounces Benton's Bacon Fat–
Washed Four Roses Bourbon
(recipe follows)
¼ ounce Grade B maple syrup
2 dashes Angostura bitters
Orange twist for garnish

Combine all ingredients except the garnish in a rocks glass filled with one large cube of ice. Stir until chilled, about 15 seconds. Garnish with the orange twist.

BENTON'S BACON FAT–WASHED
FOUR ROSES BOURBON

1½ ounces (by volume) bacon
fat rendered from Benton's
Country Bacon

750 ml bottle Four Roses
bourbon

Warm the bacon fat in a small saucepan over low heat, stirring until it is melted, about 5 minutes. Combine the melted fat with the bourbon in a large freezer-safe container and stir. Cover and let sit at room temperature for 4 hours, then place the container in the freezer for 2 hours. Remove the solid fat from the surface of the bourbon and discard. Strain the bourbon through a terry cloth towel or a double layer of cheesecloth into a bottle and store in the refrigerator for up to 2 months.

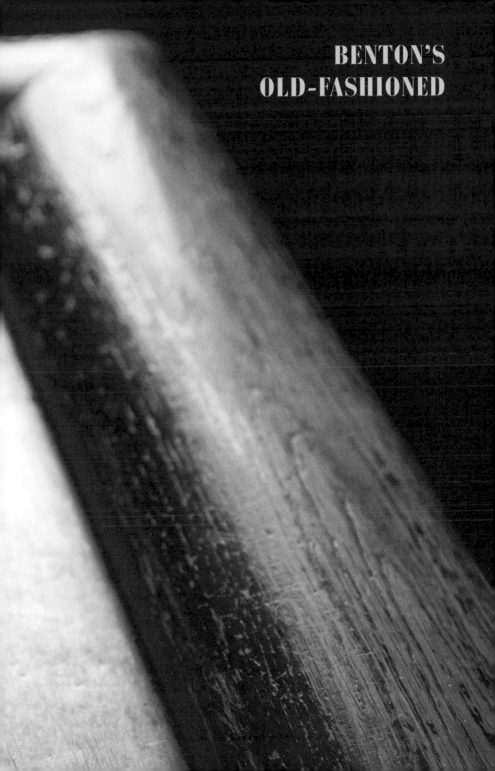

BENTON'S
OLD-FASHIONED

BITTER GIUSEPPE

The Violet Hour in Chicago seldom gets its due as a wellspring of modern classic cocktails. But no modern bar outside of the inimitable Milk & Honey and Pegu Club is better represented in this book. The Paper Plane, Eeyore's Requiem, Art of Choke, and Juliet & Romeo were all born there, as was this drink by Stephen Cole.

Cole created the drink on the spot in spring 2007 for Giuseppe Tentori, a chef he knew who wasn't much of a cocktail drinker. "Seeing how he was from Italy and preferred cocktails that were lower ABV, I thought that a Cynar-based cocktail was a good direction to start," said Cole. He began by building a Manhattan with a base of Cynar, the Italian artichoke-flavored liqueur. But, realizing that was "a horrible idea," he introduced a bit of acid through lemon juice and lemon oils to lift the drink up a bit and cut through the mixture's sweetness. He finished it off with a couple dashes of orange bitters.

The drink was slowly adopted by other bartenders who hung out at The Violet Hour. They then brought the drink back to where they worked. After a while, Cole began to see it on menus from coast to coast and even heard of appearances in France, Spain, England, and Italy.

"I think one of the keys to this cocktail is how minimal it is yet has tons of layers," he said. "Starts heavy but finishes clean."

2 ounces Cynar

¾ ounce Carpano Antica Formula vermouth

2 dashes Regans' orange bitters

Lemon peel, with a little pulp left on it

Lemon slice for garnish

Combine the liquid ingredients in a rocks glass filled with ice. Twist the lemon peel over the drink, spraying oil over the surface, with about 11 to 15 drops of lemon juice falling into the glass. Stir. Garnish with the lemon slice.

BLACK MANHATTAN

San Francisco bartender Todd Smith created this simple spin on the Manhattan while at Cortez in San Francisco in 2005. Back then, working with rye whiskey was the new frontier, the herbal Italian amaro Averna was still an oddity, and orange bitters had just come back from the dead. So this cocktail was a revelation to drinkers on three levels. Smith brought the drink with him when he opened the influential speakeasy Bourbon & Branch, thus boosting the cocktail's profile. (Several of the cocktails Bourbon & Branch became famous for, including the Revolver, were actually invented elsewhere.) But it wasn't until the late 2010s that the Black Manhattan attained ubiquity. It is now served from coast to coast by both professional and home bartenders.

2 ounces rye whiskey
1 ounce Averna
1 dash Angostura bitters
1 dash Regans' orange bitters
Cherry for garnish

Combine all ingredients except the garnish in a mixing glass half-filled with ice. Stir until chilled, about 15 seconds. Strain into a chilled coupe. Garnish with the cherry.

BRAMBLE

Dick Bradsell didn't have many fond memories of growing up on the Isle of Wight. He could not wait to flee to London, where he began what became the most celebrated bartending career in modern English history. But he did remember the fragrant blackberry patches that grew on the island. While working at the private bar Fred's Club in the early 1990s, he sampled a new crème de mure, and the taste of those wild berries came flooding back to him.

He used the liqueur to adorn a simple gin sour served on crushed ice, showing the crème de mure off properly by drizzling a half ounce of it over the top of the drink. In case people missed the point, he garnished the cocktail with a big fat blackberry. The drink made its premiere at Fred's Club, but it gained wide release when Jonathan Downey put it on the menu at his popular London bar Match, where you didn't need a membership to get in.

2 ounces gin
¾ ounce lemon juice
½ ounce simple syrup
½ ounce crème de mure
Blackberry for garnish
Lemon slice for garnish

Combine the gin, lemon juice, and simple syrup in a cocktail shaker half-filled with ice. Shake until chilled. Strain into an old-fashioned glass filled with crushed ice. Drizzle the crème de mure on top of the drink. Garnish with the blackberry and lemon slice.

BREAKFAST MARTINI

Salvatore Calabrese got the idea for his most famous cocktail, the Breakfast Martini, at, well, breakfast. One morning in 1996, Calabrese's wife, Susan, was enjoying her customary marmalade on toast. Impatient with her restless husband, who would not pause for breakfast, she insisted he sit down and have a slice himself.

"The bitter, tangy flavor of the orange marmalade played with my taste buds," recalled Calabrese, a native of Italy and by then already a veteran of the London bartending scene. At the time, he was working at the Library Bar in the Lanesborough, a luxury hotel in the city's upscale Belgravia neighborhood, just a stone's throw from Buckingham Palace. "After trying it on the toast, I took the marmalade to work with me to experiment with."

He paired a barspoon of the bittersweet jam with 1⅔ ounces of gin, in keeping with the English culinary theme. To this, he added ½ ounce each of Cointreau and lemon juice to lend the drink its sweet and fresh components, respectively. In a playful nod to the marmalade, he called the sour the Breakfast Martini.

It didn't take long for the drink to attract notice. "It was so unique and unusual that it sparked the customer's interest" almost immediately, he said. "So much so that people were asking for it as soon as we opened the bar at 11 a.m." The Breakfast Martini, it seems, was indeed a breakfast Martini from the get-go.

1⅔ ounces gin
½ ounce curaçao
½ ounce lemon juice
1 barspoon English orange marmalade
Orange twist for garnish

Combine the gin and marmalade in a cocktail shaker. Stir to dissolve the marmalade in the gin. Add the curaçao and lemon juice. Fill with ice. Shake until chilled and integrated, about 15 seconds. Fine strain into a chilled coupe. Garnish with the orange twist.

CAB CALLOWAY

Atlanta-based bartender Tiffanie Barriere, who for many years ran One Flew South—possibly the world's best airport cocktail bar—named this after the famed and flamboyant bandleader from the early twentieth century. "His style, demeanor, and performance were all the things sherry brings to the table," she said. Barriere added the drink is particularly favored by people during the holidays.

1½ ounces dark sherry, such as oloroso
½ ounce rye whiskey
¼ ounce apricot liqueur
¼ ounce dry vermouth
2 dashes Angostura bitters
2 dashes orange bitters
Lemon twist for garnish

Combine all ingredients except the garnish in a mixing glass half-filled with ice. Stir until chilled, about 15 seconds. Strain into a rocks glass filled with ice. Express the lemon twist over the surface, then drop it in.

CABLE CAR

Today, it's not uncommon to find a classic Manhattan occupying the same menu as an in-house Manhattan riff. In 1996, however, offering a modern interpretation of a nearly forgotten drink like the Sidecar was as unusual as encountering the Sidecar itself. But that's just what bartender Tony Abou-Ganim did when he dreamed up the Cable Car, which would go on to become a signature for both its creator and the place where it was born, as well as the only modern classic to showcase spiced rum.

"Back in 1996 it was still rather unique to create 'original' or 'specialty' cocktails and feature them on a menu," recalled Abou-Ganim, who worked as the head bartender at the 1920s-inspired Starlight Room when the opulent lounge was relaunched atop San Francisco's Sir Francis Drake Hotel that same year.

The seed that became the Cable Car was planted when representatives from the spiced rum brand Captain Morgan approached Abou-Ganim about developing a new drink featuring their product. A fan of the Sidecar, Abou-Ganim thought he might be able to breathe new life into the neglected classic by swapping out the base spirit of Cognac. The only other change he made was to add cinnamon to the traditional sugar rim. But those two alterations made all the difference. The cocktail was put on the Starlight Room's second menu, and quickly became a hit.

"The pairing of cinnamon sugar with a spiced rum was a simple, yet brilliant, move," said bartender Marco Dionysos, who had moved to San Francisco around that time. A few years later, in 2002, Dionysos himself was working at the Starlight. The popularity of the Cable Car had not fallen off in the least.

By then, Abou-Ganim had moved to Las Vegas. In 1998, he was tapped to operate the many bars at the sprawling Bellagio Hotel and Casino. A year-round hive of visitors, the Bellagio was an ideal forum to bring the Cable Car to a wider audience.

1½ ounces Captain Morgan
Original Spiced Rum
1 ounce lemon juice
¾ ounce curaçao
½ ounce simple syrup
1 teaspoon cinnamon
1 teaspoon sugar
1 small lemon slice
Orange twist for garnish

In a small shallow bowl, mix the cinnamon and sugar. Wet the edge of a chilled cocktail glass with the lemon slice and dip the rim in the sugar mixture. Combine the liquid ingredients in a cocktail shaker half-filled with ice. Shake until chilled, about 15 seconds. Strain into the prepared glass. Garnish with the orange twist.

CE SOIR

Boston bartender Nicole Lebedevitch had a regular at Eastern Standard named Nate who always ordered Manhattans. To entertain him, she began making every conceivable variation on the drink, trying different modifiers and bitters.

"Nate joined us for his bachelor party dinner with about sixteen friends and did the ol' 'You know what I like' for their last round of drinks as they headed out to the patio," remembered Lebedevitch. "I guess it was the allure of the cigars, but this was this first time I grabbed Cognac as the base, and then it was to reach for the honeyed flavor of yellow Chartreuse, the bitterness of Cynar, and the salt and pepper of the combination of the Angostura and Regans' orange bitters."

The result was Ce Soir. She continued to tweak the drink and brought it over to Eastern Standard's sister bar, The Hawthorne. There she was introduced to 1840 Pierre Ferrand Cognac, and that became the new base. Ce Soir landed on the menu at The Hawthorne in 2011 and became a popular order with regulars. So successful in its simplicity and marriage of strong, sturdy flavors, it deserves a wider audience.

2 ounces Cognac, preferably
Pierre Ferrand 1840
Original Formula
¾ ounce Cynar
½ yellow Chartreuse
1 dash Angostura bitters
1 dash Regans' orange bitters
Lemon twist

Combine all ingredients except the lemon twist in a mixing glass half-filled with ice. Stir until chilled. Strain into a chilled cocktail glass. Express the lemon twist over the surface of the drink and discard.

CHARTREUSE SWIZZLE

In the San Francisco bar world of the early aughts, it was all about Fernet and Chartreuse. Those were the two prevailing "bartender's handshakes"—under-the-radar spirits enjoyed by mixologists who prided themselves on their connoisseurship.

Marcovaldo Dionysos was a Chartreuse soldier—so much so that for five years running he entered a San Francisco cocktail competition sponsored by the French herbal liqueur. Over the first four contests, he won once and placed second or third the other times. Having achieved this respectable record as a Chartreuse master, he was prepared to sit out the fifth competition in 2002. But the event organizer reached out and asked him to reconsider.

Dionysos's entry was the Chartreuse Swizzle, an improbable drink that dragged the centuries-old European liqueur into the realm of tiki. He paired it with pineapple juice, lime juice, mint, a load of ice, and one other secret ingredient that all but stole the show from the bright green elixir. Dionysos remembered reading about Velvet falernum, a spiced syrup from the Caribbean, and was intrigued. Once a popular cocktail ingredient, it had been all but forgotten by the twenty-first century until Dale DeGroff created a few cocktails with the syrup and promoted it as well.

Between the falernum and the drink's exotic form—swizzles, icy concoctions typically made with rum and associated with the Caribbean, were not well known in the States at the time—Dionysos caught the judges' fancy. He took home the prize—a Fuji mountain bike, as he remembered.

Thereafter commenced the Chartreuse Swizzle's incremental, decade-long climb to worldwide recognition. The Swizzle made its first menu appearance at Harry Denton's Starlight Room, a swank drinkery where Dionysos was working. Denton, a renowned lover of Chartreuse who was known to pour shots of the stuff for guests, was a receptive audience. The cocktail sold decently but was hardly setting the room on fire.

It was at the Clock Bar that the cocktail took off. The boîte was opened by celebrity chef Michael Mina in 2008. Clock Bar got plenty of press attention, and the Chartreuse Swizzle was on the opening menu. The cocktail also appeared at Bourbon & Branch, which, upon opening in 2006, instantly became the most famous craft cocktail bar in the city.

"Marco's cocktail seemed to pop up on the most random cocktail menus in town," recalled cocktail writer Camper English, "and to this day, any time someone combines Chartreuse and pineapple juice, nerds are obligated to scream, 'So it's basically a Chartreuse Swizzle without the falernum?'"

Beginning around 2010, the drink grew international legs. Dionysos partly credits the complex base spirit for the cocktail's enduring popularity. "Chartreuse is magical stuff," he said. "I think this drink tastes enough of Chartreuse to satisfy die-hard fans of the spirit but softens it enough to attract newbies." The drink is also easy to put together. It has only four ingredients, and, now that falernum is a more common commodity, none of them are hard to find. Still, while the drink may be simple to make, it never tastes like a simple drink.

1½ ounces green Chartreuse
1 ounce pineapple juice
¾ ounce lime juice
½ ounce Velvet falernum
Mint sprig for garnish
Freshly grated nutmeg for garnish

Combine all ingredients except the garnishes in a cocktail shaker half-filled with ice. Shake until chilled, about 15 seconds. Strain into a collins glass filled with ice. Garnish with the mint sprig and nutmeg.

CIA

Can a shot be a classic cocktail? Ever heard of a Kamikaze? Or a B-52? Of course, any shooter that came of age during the cocktail renaissance is going to be less louche. Tonia Guffey's CIA is made up of Cynar, the heritage artichoke liquor from Italy, and Laird's bonded apple brandy—two products with unassailable pedigrees. Guffey, a bartender at Dram in Brooklyn and Flatiron Lounge in Manhattan in the early 2010s, was inspired to concoct the potion by a very mixological motivation: she was drinking too much Fernet Branca and needed a change.

"I wanted to switch from Fernet to shots of Cynar, but to be honest, it didn't pack the punch I wanted. I adored Laird's bonded and the proof was there, so one night I decided to cut the Cynar with Laird's to give it some oomph. It was pretty fucking delicious." The idea of inventing a shooter was not anathema to her. "Back in my early club bar days I probably poured and drank a thousand Red-Headed Slut shots [Jägermeister, peach schnapps, and cranberry juice]," she said, "so maybe some underlying inspiration was there." She eventually tweaked it by adding a dash of Angostura bitters.

Still, one doesn't put shooters on menus at cocktail bars, no matter how delicious. So this one built an underground reputation as a "bartender's handshake," something Guffey would pour for fellow barkeeps as they congregated at Dram after their shifts ended at other bars. "It was cheap, easy, and packed a wallop, so it was perfect," said Guffey. (Guffey called it the Dram shot or sometimes Triple A for amaro, Ango, and applejack. The CIA name—"Cynar In Applejack"—was bestowed by bartender Sother Teague of Amor y Amargo.)

Word of the shot spread farther when Guffey and her fellow Dram bartenders would order the drink at bars in New Orleans and Boston and Philadelphia. Most bars they visited had all three ingredients, so it was an easy call. Guffey knew it had achieved a certain fame when she visited a San Diego bar one day and the bartender poured her a CIA, asking if she had ever heard of it.

"No one believes me when I say I created it," said Guffey.

½ ounce Cynar
½ ounce Laird's bonded apple brandy
1 dash Angostura bitters

Build the ingredients in a shot glass and serve.

CORPSE REVIVER NO. BLUE

Can a joke cocktail be a classic? Is Tom Collins running around town badmouthing you? Did Harvey Wallbanger run for president?

In other words: Yes, it can.

In 2006, Jacob Briars, a bartender from New Zealand, was organizing a cocktail competition in Queenstown. During the run-up, one of the competing bartenders, obsessed with the pre-Prohibition drink Corpse Reviver No. 2, kept ordering it around town. At the same time, a spirits order for the contest went awry and Briars ended up with two *cases* of blue curaçao. This put Briars in mind of the Facebook rantings of high-strung mixologists who called themselves "Jihad on Blue Drinks."

Cocktail bartenders weren't known for their sense of humor back then. Briars, feeling that that balloon of hot air needed some puncturing, took some of the extra blue curaçao and, on the final evening of the competition, whipped up a Corpse Reviver No. Blue—basically the same drink, but of a different color.

Briars's witty jibe struck the right note at the time. "People didn't like blue drinks, or at least thought they shouldn't like blue drinks," he recalled. It also helps that the cocktail, while looking like a disco drink, tasted like something from the golden age.

Sebastian Reaburn, at 1806 bar in Melbourne, was the first person to serve Briars his own drink. Soon it was all over New Zealand and Australia. A year later, Briars was being tagged on Facebook whenever the cocktail was served in a bar. The free-flowing exchange of bartending talent between Australia and the UK quickly brought the drink to London, where it was served at no-less-lauded a place than Milk & Honey.

Briars correctly points out that the drink accomplished nothing new in terms of flavor or structure. Its role was more behavioral. It reminded bartenders that they could be serious about their craft and have a little fun at the same time.

1 ounce gin
1 ounce Lillet Blanc
1 ounce blue curaçao
1 ounce lemon juice
1 dash absinthe
Lemon twist for garnish

Combine all ingredients except the garnish in a cocktail shaker half-filled with ice. Shake until chilled, about 15 seconds. Strain into a chilled coupe and garnish with the lemon twist.

COSMOPOLITAN

Looking at the arc of the cocktail revival, the Cosmopolitan is well outside the scope of most of the cocktails in this book, which are largely children of the twenty-first century. The Cosmo was invented way back in 1988. But despite being rather long in the tooth, it counts as a modern classic for two reasons: it is easily the most famous cocktail to have come along in what can generously be termed recent times, and it's the cocktail that helped the concept of the cocktail remain relevant at a time when most people didn't care whether the Great American Mixed Drink lived or died.

Bartender Toby Cecchini invented this simple sour as a shift drink for the staff at Odeon, which then was about the hottest chop house in town thanks to the literary Brat Pack. The arrival of Absolut Citron (flavored vodka was not as played out then as it is now) and news of a worse drink with the same name circulating in San Francisco circles served as his initial inspiration. The drink took off rather quickly. Being featured by Dale DeGroff at the Rainbow Room helped. Being chosen as the whistle-wetter of choice of the quartet of would-be Holly Golightlys at the center of *Sex and the City* helped even more. When highbrow mixology came into vogue, the Cosmo was rejected as a relic of the bad old days. But in time, young bartenders got off their high horse and heeded Marshall Field's timeless advice to give the people what they want.

As often happens when a drink is wildly successful, a good number of claim jumpers said they had invented the Cosmo. As a result, most accounts of the Cosmo's history refer to a "controversy" over the drink's origins. This "both sides" school of cocktail historicism serves the public no better than the same approach does political journalism. Cecchini currently owns Long Island Bar in Brooklyn. If you go there, you won't find the Cosmo on the menu. But they keep cranberry juice behind the bar just in case.

---

2 ounces Absolut Citron vodka
1 ounce Cointreau
1 ounce lime juice
1 ounce Ocean Spray Cranberry Cocktail
Lemon twist for garnish

Combine all ingredients except the garnish in a cocktail shaker half-filled with ice. Shake until chilled, about 15 seconds. Strain into a chilled coupe. Garnish with the lemon twist.

DEATH FLIP

The Death Flip is testimony to the continuing appeal of the barroom dare. When the cocktail first appeared on the menu at the Black Pearl bar in Melbourne, in 2010, no ingredients were listed. If you asked what was in the drink, the bartender would not tell you. The only thing giving the customer a hint as to what they were getting into was the line "You don't wanna meet this cocktail in a dark alley."

Of course, plenty of people took the bait, and many ended up liking the cocktail. That probably wouldn't have happened if the Black Pearl had advertised the ingredients: tequila, yellow Chartreuse, Jägermeister, and a whole egg. Taken together, the mélange was downright intimidating.

"You know how it is," said Chris Hysted-Adams, explaining how he came to create the Death Flip. "You're a young, impressionable bartender, so all you like drinking is tequila, Jägermeister, and Chartreuse. Chances are, during service, you're recommending cocktails to your guests with tequila, Jägermeister, or Chartreuse in them."

The problem is, customers don't like such pet bar-world spirits as much as bartenders do. Frustrated by his clientele's timidity, Hysted-Adams doubled down on his preferences and created a drink that included all three spirits. It didn't take long for it to develop a cult following. "They'd have a sip, and the look on their face was priceless," recalled Hysted-Adams. "They couldn't believe that car crash of ingredients tasted so good." Shortly after, he had bartender acquaintances emailing him, asking for permission to feature it on their cocktail lists.

As for the impression-making name, the drink is indeed a flip—that is, the nineteenth-century genre of cocktail that calls for an egg. But there is a second meaning. "I'm a skateboarding tragic, and the death flip is a bad-ass trick," said Hysted. "A drink this bad-ass needed a bad-ass name to go with it."

---

1 ounce blanco tequila
½ ounce yellow Chartreuse
½ ounce Jägermeister
1 dash simple syrup
1 whole egg
Freshly grated nutmeg
for garnish

Combine all ingredients except the garnish in a cocktail shaker half-filled with ice. Shake vigorously. Strain into a sour glass. Garnish with nutmeg.

DEMOCRAT

San Francisco bartender Jon Santer was reading a biography of Harry Truman when he came up with this highball in 2007. According to the book, the thirty-third U.S. president and his wife would routinely enjoy a glass of bourbon, either neat or with a splash, every evening on the porch of their Missouri home.

"I wanted to make a drink to honor him, as I feel like he's a wildly underrated president who faced impossible odds and had to make some of the hardest decisions of anyone, ever," said Santer. "I obviously couldn't just start calling bourbon neat a 'Truman,' though that would be a trick. So I started to think about great porch drinks, things one could sip on while enjoying the Missouri evening light. The Democrat to me is a kind of boozy sweet tea/lemonade. Like an Arnold Palmer."

2 ounces bourbon
¾ ounce lemon juice
½ ounce peach liqueur
½ ounce honey syrup (1:1)
Lemon wheel for garnish
Mint sprig for garnish

Combine all ingredients except the garnishes in a cocktail shaker half-filled with ice. Give it a short shake, about 5 seconds. Strain into a collins glass filled with pebble ice. Add more ice and a straw. Garnish with the lemon wheel and mint sprig.

DIVISION BELL

Bartender Phil Ward already had a few noteworthy cocktail creations under his belt when he came up with this early mezcal classic for the opening 2009 menu at Mayahuel, his pioneering agave-focused East Village bar—which turned out to be the only bar Ward ever owned. (He has since sworn off bar ownership, happy to spend his remaining days as a humble barkeep.) The drink is a fairly simple twist on the Last Word, a lost pre-Prohibition cocktail that inspired many young bartenders in the aughts. Ward replaced the gin in the Last Word with mezcal. And instead of Chartreuse, he reached for Aperol, an easygoing Italian bitters that was then winning friends left and right. The drink was an early favorite with Mayahuel guests and one of the bar's best sellers. The recipe has since appeared in nearly every published book about agave spirits.

Ward named the drink after a Pink Floyd album he listened to a lot while staining the wooden surfaces of the bar prior to Mayahuel's opening. He recalled that bar build-out as one of the most stressful things he's ever gone through. A cold Division Bell is a perfect remedy for such stress.

1 ounce mezcal, preferably Del Maguey Vida
¾ ounce Aperol
¾ ounce lime juice
½ ounce maraschino liqueur
Grapefruit twist

Combine all ingredients except the twist in a cocktail shaker half-filled with ice. Shake until chilled, about 15 seconds. Strain into a chilled coupe. Express the grapefruit twist over the drink and discard the peel.

EARL GREY MARTEANI

Audrey Saunders's American creation—spelled, with punning emphasis, as Earl Grey MarTEAni—actually made its debut in London in 2003, at a pop-up at the Ritz's Rivoli Bar. That was appropriate, since the cocktail was intended as an homage to the hotel's legendary tea service. "Tea is often served with lemon, lumps of sugar on the side, and milk," explained Saunders. "Instead of using milk, I opted for the egg white, which not only provides an ethereal mouthfeel but is also a perfect foil for the tea's tannins. Technically the egg white bonds to the tannins in the tea before it has an opportunity to cause palate fatigue, similar to what you might experience with red wine. The half-sugar rim is a nod to the lumps of sugar traditionally served with tea."

The drink made its American debut at the Bemelmans Bar in the Carlyle, where Saunders worked at the time. Still later it became a staple at Pegu Club, the bar Saunders ran in Manhattan.

1½ ounces Earl Grey Tea-Infused Tanqueray Gin (recipe follows)

1 ounce simple syrup

¾ ounce lemon juice

1 egg white

Sugar for the rim

Lemon wedge for the rim and a twist for garnish

Wet half of the rim of a chilled cocktail glass with the lemon wedge and dip the rim in sugar. Combine the liquid ingredients and egg white in a cocktail shaker. Shake briefly without ice, about 10 seconds. Fill the shaker half-full with ice. Shake until chilled, about 15 seconds. Strain into the prepared glass. Garnish with the lemon twist.

EARL GREY TEA–INFUSED TANQUERAY GIN

---

1 cup Tanqueray gin

1 tablespoon loose Earl Grey tea leaves

Combine the ingredients in a bottle. Stir briefly and gently. Infuse for 2 hours. Fine strain the tea leaves from the gin. The infusion will keep at room temperature for 2 days.

EEYORE'S REQUIEM

"How much bitters can you throw at just one drink?" asked one magazine about the Eeyore's Requiem.

As far as bartender Toby Maloney was concerned, a lot. The cocktail, created for an early menu at Chicago's The Violet Hour, contained not only Campari but also Cynar and Fernet Branca. Together they comprise two ounces of booze and pointedly shift the lesser amounts of gin and blanc vermouth to the backseat.

"We had been really pushing the envelope on what makes a Negroni," said Maloney. "Even our house Negroni was two ounces gin, one ounce sweet vermouth, a half ounce Campari, and three dashes orange bitters. So this was looking to completely turn that on its head and make it a Campari-based cocktail while stacking complexity and bitterness to the nth degree."

Predictably, chefs and bartenders cottoned to it. As that magazine item pointed out, it was "one for the geeks." But eventually, as Negroni riffs and amari began to rise in popularity, it gathered a wider audience.

Looking back, though, Maloney thinks he may have gotten the name wrong. "Naming a drink after a beloved children's book character is kind of a bait and switch. Eeyore is cute even while being melancholy. This drink is not cute."

1½ ounces Campari
1 ounce Dolin blanc vermouth
½ ounce gin
¼ ounce Cynar
¼ ounce Fernet Branca
1 dash Angostura orange bitters
1 dash Regan's orange bitters
Orange twist for garnish

Combine all ingredients except the garnish in a mixing glass half-filled with ice. Stir until chilled, about 15 seconds. Strain into a chilled coupe. Garnish with the orange twist.

ELLISON

Charles Hardwick, the beverage director at Blue Owl, a small cocktail bar in New York's East Village, was a fan of both novelist Ralph Ellison and Hendrick's gin, an unusual Scottish gin launched at the dawn of the twenty-first century that for a time was catnip for cocktail bartenders. The result of those two passions was the Ellison, a 2006 spin on the Southside cocktail that threw in muddled cucumber to echo the cucumber flavors in the gin. (Hendrick's can be credited with the flurry of cocktails created in the aughts that called for cucumber, an ingredient that previously not had much play in mixology outside of the Pimm's Cup.)

"It was immediately a hit with everyone," recalled Hardwick. "I've never served a drink with broader appeal—women, men, older, millennials, bartenders, and everyday guests all loved it." Hardwick went on to work at some of New York's best bars, including the Grill and the Office. But this early drink remains Hardwick's best-known creation. "I still think it's a very important drink in my career," he said, "and it represents a certain style of drink, and its time and place, very well."

1½ ounces gin, preferably Hendrick's
¾ ounce lime juice
½ ounce simple syrup
2 dashes Angostura bitters
4 or 5 mint leaves
6 thin slices of cucumber

Muddle the lime juice, simple syrup, mint leaves, and 3 of the cucumber slices at the bottom of a cocktail shaker. Add the gin and bitters. Fill with ice. Shake until chilled, about 15 seconds. Fine strain into a chilled cocktail glass. Garnish with the remaining 3 cucumber slices.

FITZGERALD

Joe Baum, the restaurant mastermind behind the 1980s rebirth of the Rainbow Room, didn't want any original cocktails on the drink menu. But that didn't stop customers from asking head bartender Dale DeGroff to make them custom concoctions. And once one patron got an off-menu treat, others got wind of it and wanted one as well.

One night in 1995, a jaded gin-and-tonic drinker asked DeGroff for something with a bit more pizzazz. DeGroff fixed up a basic gin sour—gin, lemon juice, and simple syrup—and topped it with a few shakes of Angostura bitters. He then shook it up and served it on the rocks with a lemon wheel garnish. The guy ordered several of them.

Soon people were asking for "the gin thing." The cocktail became the sensation of the summer of 1995, and DeGroff finally decided to put it on the menu. There was already a Hemingway Daiquiri on the list. A bar regular who was a writer at the *New Yorker* thought it only fair that the new drink be named after Hemingway's contemporary and literary rival, F. Scott. Thus, the Fitzgerald was born. (Having both novelists on the menu gave bartenders a good lead-in to a story with customers, said DeGroff.)

The media soon picked up on the new drink, and when DeGroff included it in his 2002 book, *The Craft of the Cocktail*, all the world was in on the secret. It continues to be popular at bars around the world. But if you really want to find the cocktail's home, visit St. Paul, Fitzgerald's hometown, and its sister city, Minneapolis. There's hardly a cocktail bar in the city that doesn't proudly serve it.

1½ ounces gin
1 ounce simple syrup
¾ ounce lemon juice
2 dashes Angostura bitters
Lemon slice for garnish

Combine all ingredients except the garnish in a cocktail shaker half-filled with ice. Shake until chilled, about 15 seconds. Strain into a chilled rocks glass. Garnish with the lemon slice.

FRENCH PEARL

One of the central missions of Pegu Club, the New York bar that Audrey Saunders ran from 2005 to 2020, was to change customers' ingrained drinking habits, or at least open customers up to new cocktails and spirits. In 2006, few people in the United States saw the appeal of gin or pastis. Saunders's rather counterintuitive solution to this problem was to put both gin and pastis in the same shaken drink—along with lime juice, simple syrup, and mint leaves.

The name references both the popularity of pastis in late 1800s France and the opalescent quality created when the pastis louched in the glass, an effect Saunders considered the drink's "garnish."

The French Pearl debuted on the Pegu menu in spring 2006. It was yet another in a line of Saunders's Mojito explorations, which previously included the Gin-Gin Mule (page 70) and the Old Cuban (page 111). The French Pearl took a bit longer to take off, as Saunders was busy running a bar and had no time for travel to promote the drink internationally. But it had its ardent following, and in recent years that slow-burn fan base has paid off, belatedly bestowing fame upon the drink.

2 ounces gin
¾ ounce lime juice
¾ ounce simple syrup
¼ ounce Pernod
6 mint leaves

Combine the lime juice, simple syrup, and mint leaves in a cocktail shaker. Gently muddle the mint leaves. Add the gin, Pernod, and ice to the shaker. Shake until chilled, about 15 seconds. Fine strain into a chilled coupe.

GIN BASIL SMASH

The most famous modern classic cocktail to come out of Germany was conceived one night in 2007 when Joerg Meyer, owner of the Hamburg speakeasy Le Lion, was having a drink at Pegu Club, one of the best cocktail bars in New York. He ordered the Whiskey Smash—a mix of bourbon, simple syrup, lemon juice, and muddled mint created by Dale DeGroff. The drink immediately lodged in his mind.

Back in Germany the next year, at an industry workshop, Meyer was paging through a recipe booklet provided by a brand rep for G'Vine, the French gin. An unusual basil garnish featured in the book caught his attention. That same evening, as was his habit, Meyer preceded his nightly shift with an espresso at the nearby Café Paris. There he often chatted with the chefs and borrowed ingredients to experiment with at Le Lion. Thinking of the mint in DeGroff's Whiskey Smash, as well as the garnish in the G'Vine manual, he grabbed a bunch of fresh basil that night. He tried it first with bourbon, using the Smash formula. Not delicious. Then he tried gin, and voilà!

Over the next few years—through a combination of the drink's natural appeal, a post on Meyer's well-read cocktail blog *The Bitters Blog*, and Meyer's innate talent for self-promotion—the drink became a hit in Germany. Soon after, it jumped the border and was served in other countries. In 2012, Meyer painted the words "Cradle of the Gin Basil Smash" on the outside of his bar.

Meyer sells 300 to 500 Gin Basil Smashes at Le Lion every week, 22,000 annually, and the bar goes through more than 3,100 bottles of gin every year. The drink is so ubiquitous that a bartender once called it "Meyer's curse." Bartenders hate muddling.

2 ounces gin
1 ounce lemon juice
¾ ounce simple syrup
2 sprigs of basil leaves

Muddle one sprig of basil leaves at the bottom of a cocktail shaker. Add the other ingredients and fill with ice. Shake until chilled, about 15 seconds. Double strain into a rocks glass filled with ice. Garnish with the remaining basil sprig.

GIN BLOSSOM

In 2009, when Julie Reiner was preparing to open Clover Club, her populist Brooklyn cocktail bar, she knew she wanted to offer a house Manhattan and a house Martini that weren't *exactly* a Manhattan and a Martini. The former emerged as the Slope (page 133), the latter as the Gin Blossom. The key ingredient distinguishing both was a single flavor: apricot.

Eric Seed, of the Minnesota-based importer Haus Alpenz, had just introduced Reiner to his new-to-market apricot eau de vie and apricot liqueur. Reiner thought that they were both excellent and might work in riffs on classics.

She tinkered with the Gin Blossom at Flatiron Lounge, her Manhattan cocktail bar. Reiner ran through countless permutations of gin, vermouth, and bitters for a test audience of friends and colleagues. The final recipe harkened back to early mixological history, which had a long tradition of adding trace amounts of an ingredient or two to the classic combination of gin and vermouth.

The Gin Blossom was an immediate hit with guests. Among its early fans was one person very close to the drink's creator: Susan Fedroff, co-owner of Clover Club and Reiner's wife. Fedroff wasn't expecting to be won over. "I was never much of a gin drinker; I like whiskey," Fedroff said. "But it is legitimately one of my favorite drinks of all time."

She wasn't alone. During those early days, Fedroff was in the habit of checking the Clover Club sales report at the end of the day. "It was all about the Gin Blossoms and deviled eggs," she remembers.

1½ ounces Plymouth gin
1½ ounces Martini
bianco vermouth
¾ ounce apricot eau de vie
2 dashes orange bitters
Orange twist for garnish

Combine all ingredients except the garnish in a mixing glass half-filled with ice and stir until chilled, about 15 seconds. Strain into a chilled coupe. Garnish with the orange twist.

GIN-GIN MULE

This cocktail is the crowning achievement, in gin terms, of early gin advocate Audrey Saunders. It is essentially a Mojito (a rum drink) crossed with a Moscow Mule (a vodka drink), but made with gin. It also illustrates the wide influence the omnipresent Mojito had on bartenders at the turn of the twenty-first century.

"Dale [DeGroff] showed me his recipe for a classic Mojito with a dash or two of Angostura," said Saunders. "Having a cocktail that had a fresh herb in it—who knew? Wow, that's amazing. For me, the Mojito base, mint and lime, was really, really enjoyable. At that point, I dove head first into gin. So, sub out the rum and try the gin and see how that tastes."

Saunders found a recipe for homemade ginger beer from a kitchen staff member at Beacon, the midtown Manhattan restaurant where she managed the bar. "It had a lot more sugar in it, so I tightened it up," said Saunders, who reasoned that she was already adding simple syrup in cocktails anyway. The drink debuted at Beacon in 2000. It later became a mainstay at Pegu Club, Saunders' lower Manhattan cocktail bar.

(Saunders believes that the key to this drink is the homemade ginger beer, since store-bought ginger beer has a more peppery than gingery profile and is many times more sweet. So making the ginger beer is worth your while. If you absolutely must use commercial ginger beer, reduce the simple syrup in the drink to ½ ounce or less.)

1¾ ounces Tanqueray gin
1 ounce simple syrup
1 ounce homemade Ginger Beer
(recipe follows)
¾ ounce lime juice
2 mint sprigs
Lime wheel for garnish
Candied ginger for garnish

Combine the simple syrup, lime juice, and one mint sprig at the bottom of a cocktail glass. Muddle well. Add the gin and ginger beer and half-fill with ice. Shake until chilled, about 15 seconds. Strain into a highball glass filled with ice. Garnish with the remaining mint sprig, lime wheel, and candied ginger. Serve with a straw.

GINGER BEER

1 quart filtered water

4 ounces finely chopped fresh ginger

1 ounce light brown sugar

½ ounce lime juice

Add the water to a pot and bring to a boil. Put the ginger root in a food processor. Add 1 cup of the boiling water to the ginger to make processing easier. Process until coarsely ground. Return the ginger to the remaining boiling water and turn off the heat. Stir well, then cover and let sit for 1 hour. Strain through a fine chinois or cheesecloth, pressing down firmly on the ginger to extract the most flavor. Add the brown sugar and lime juice. Let cool. Transfer to glass bottles and store in the refrigerator. Ginger beer will keep for 2 weeks.

GOLD RUSH

The Gold Rush, invented by T. J. Siegal, was the first breakout original cocktail at Milk & Honey, the holy of holies of modern cocktail bars. Siegal's achievement is all the more remarkable when you consider that he's not really a bartender. In fact, he came up with the idea for the Gold Rush not while standing behind the bar at Milk & Honey, but while sitting at it, sometime in 2000.

"I had finished a long shift at work in midtown," told Siegal, "and I sat down for a bourbon sour as I had many nights previous—on the rocks, without egg or garnish." Milk & Honey founder Sasha Petraske, who also happened to be Siegal's childhood friend, told him about a honey syrup he had put together to make an old drink called the Honeysuckle Cocktail (basically a Daiquiri made with honey). Siegal asked him to make his Bourbon Sour with that honey syrup instead of simple syrup. The bourbon used was Knob Creek; later, Elijah Craig 12-year-old would be used.

"It was right the first time," recalled Siegal of the drink. He christened it the Gold Rush.

Milk & Honey famously lacked a menu back then. Drink orders were arrived at through a conversation between the server and customer. Soon the Gold Rush was being suggested to whiskey lovers. By early 2002, it was a staple at the bar.

The key to the drink is the sweetener, and not just because it's honey. The honey syrup was not a simple equal-parts affair; it was a rich syrup, made of three parts honey and one part water. The result, as far as the Gold Rush was concerned, was a Whiskey Sour so silky and deeply flavored that it led to an "aha!" moment for many people not yet sold on the culinary possibilities of a craft cocktail.

The Gold Rush would eventually be surpassed as Milk & Honey's most famous creation by the Penicillin (page 114), another Whiskey Sour variation. But Siegal can take a little credit there as well, because the Penicillin (made of blended scotch, lemon juice, honey-ginger syrup, and a float of single-malt Scotch whisky) was partly inspired by the Gold Rush.

CONTINUED >

Bartender Theo Lieberman added his own tweak when, in 2010, he invented what he called the "regal shake," in which he shook up sours with a piece of grapefruit peel. "Not only did it totally change the flavor profile, it would also change the texture," said Lieberman. The Gold Rush responded beautifully to the technique. "It really helps with anything with honey in it, because it cuts the sweetness and richness."

2 ounces bourbon
¾ ounce lemon juice
¾ ounce rich honey syrup (3:1)

Combine the ingredients in a cocktail shaker half-filled with ice. Shake until chilled, about 15 seconds. Strain into an old-fashioned glass filled with one large ice cube.

GREENPOINT

The Greenpoint is the most famous and successful of the many Manhattan/ Brooklyn riffs inspired in the late aughts by Vincenzo Errico's Red Hook cocktail (page 124). Michael McIlroy, the drink's father, is an Irishman who worked alongside Errico at New York's famous Milk & Honey. Wanting to come up with his own "neighborhood cocktail," he drew on the Brooklyn area where he then lived, Greenpoint, and the famously green French liqueur, Chartreuse. McIlroy ended up using yellow Chartreuse in the version that finally hit the bar but kept the name anyway.

2 ounces rye
½ ounce yellow Chartreuse
½ ounce sweet vermouth
1 dash Angostura bitters
1 dash orange bitters
Lemon twist for garnish

Combine all ingredients except the garnish in a mixing glass half-filled with ice. Stir until chilled, about 15 seconds. Strain into a chilled coupe. Garnish with the lemon twist.

GUNSHOP FIZZ

The Gunshop Fizz is the only well-known cocktail to use large amounts of Peychaud's bitters, the bright-red bitters used primarily to complete a Sazerac and, until recently, sold mainly in New Orleans. The drink was created by Kirk Estopinal and Maksym Pazuniak, two New Orleans bartenders who worked at Cure, the first major craft cocktail bar to open in the city.

Estopinal had worked at The Violet Hour in Chicago, where he retreated after the devastation of Hurricane Katrina in 2005. There he served The Violet Hour version of the Pimm's Cup (a favorite drink at the legendary New Orleans bar Napoleon House), which called for muddled strawberries and cucumbers. Estopinal and Pazuniak took that formula and, quite quixotically, substituted Peychaud's for the Pimm's—two liquids that have very little in common except that their ingredient lists are secret and they are bright red. A few more tweaks—including the addition of yet another ruby beverage, the nonalcoholic Italian aperitivo Sanbitter—and they arrived at the Gunshop Fizz. The creation of the drink helped lead to the publication of *Rogue Cocktails*, a 2009 collection of similarly unorthodox cocktails. Because of the drink's costliness, it is not widely served, but within cocktail circles it is known.

2 ounces Peychaud's bitters
1 ounce lemon juice
1 ounce simple syrup
2 strawberries
3 cucumber slices
3 swaths of grapefruit peel
3 swaths of orange peel
1 ounce Sanbitter
Cucumber slice for garnish

Muddle all ingredients except the Sanbitter and cucumber garnish at the bottom of a cocktail shaker. Let sit for 2 minutes to allow the flavors to mingle. Add ice. Shake until chilled, about 15 seconds. Strain into a collins glass filled with ice. Top with Sanbitter. Garnish with the cucumber slice.

HARD START

Fernet Branca was a great muse to many in the early years of the cocktail revival. An ancient liqueur, strongly flavored, bitter, and difficult to like, it checked a lot of boxes for brash young mixologists. One of them was Damon Boelte, who learned of Fernet while working at the legendary Brooklyn liquor store LeNell's. He applied those lessons when, in 2009, he was appointed beverage director at Prime Meats in the same borough. Boelte had ambitions to create a cocktail that had the most Fernet in it. He first achieved this goal with a drink called the Waterfront, which contained a whopping three ounces of the stuff. The drink started out as a mix of Branca Menta (Fernet's minty counterpart), lime, and ginger ale. From there, it evolved into a split-based mule of sorts, with a 2:1 ratio of Fernet Branca to Branca Menta, and lime, ginger beer, and mint. The Waterfront enjoyed steady popularity at Prime Meats, but it was its abbreviated child that would achieve true fame.

In the middle of a brutal brunch service one morning, Boelte's general manager, Bill, asked him for something to ease the pain. Boelte grabbed both Branca Menta and Fernet Branca and poured them into two small rocks glasses. After drinking his, Bill came back to the bar and asked, "Hey man, what the fuck was that?!" Boelte replied that it was "a Waterfront without all the bullshit in it." When Bill said the effect of the shot reminded him of when you roll a motorcycle downhill and pop the clutch to get it going, Boelte christened the drink the Hard Start.

Word of the secret shot spread quickly. Soon it was put on the dessert menu as an after-dinner drink. But people ordered it at all times of day. When Boelte left Prime Meats to open Grand Army in 2015 nearby, the drink followed him and sold just as well. The drink's notoriety was pushed along by its portability. A Hard Start can be mixed up anywhere Fernet is sold (which is nearly everywhere).

"It travels well as a boomerang," said Boelte, mentioning the clandestine habit bartenders have of sending fellow barkeeps single-serving cocktails from one bar to another. "I even sent a Hard Start hidden in an [miniature] Underberg bottle to Bill after he moved to Texas. I heard he cried."

½ ounce Fernet Branca
½ ounce Branca Menta

Combine the ingredients in a shot glass and serve.

JASMINE

The Jasmine is one of the earliest entries in the modern classic cocktail canon, coming just a couple of years after the creation of the Cosmopolitan (with which it shares a pink hue and to which it is often compared) and just as bartender Dale DeGroff, an acknowledged founder of the cocktail renaissance, was beginning to earn a reputation for liquid wizardry at New York's Rainbow Room. In fact, DeGroff played an indirect role in the creation of the Jasmine.

In 1989, chef Evelyne Slomon had just moved to Berkeley and was looking for a place to find a good cocktail. In New York she had been spoiled by her friend DeGroff, who had tested all his Rainbow Room creations on her. While visiting friends at a restaurant in Emeryville, she discovered Townhouse, a former speakeasy that had recently been refurbished and reopened by Joseph LeBrun. She quickly became a regular. She taught novice bartender Paul Harrington how to make a Martini the way she liked it. Many cocktail-oriented discussions followed.

Townhouse had no cocktail menu. Harrington got in the habit of asking customers what they liked to drink and what they were in the mood for. Acting on that information, he chose a drink for them from the existing catalog of cocktails.

The Jasmine came about one slow weekday night when Matt Jasmin, an infrequent guest at Townhouse, walked in. He asked Harrington to make him something he had never made before. In Harrington's recently acquired copy of *Trader Vic's Bartender's Guide*, he'd read about the Pegu Club, an old pre-Prohibition drink made of gin, curaçao, lime juice, and bitters.

Staring at his backbar that night, his gaze fell on the Campari bottle. "I used to make my Pegu with a fair amount of bitters," said Harrington, "so when I eyed the Campari, a light went on, and I thought I could make a substitution." A full basket of fresh lemons on the bar inspired him to replace the Pegu's lime juice with lemon juice and garnish the drink with a lemon twist. He named it after Jasmin. (Harrington did not discover until many years later that he had misspelled his friend's name, which lacks an "e." By then it was too late; the "Jasmine" it was.)

During the 1990s, Harrington connected with some editors of the then-new magazine *Wired*, and they collaborated on CocktailTime.com, a series of cocktail columns that ran on Wired's new website, Hotwired.com. In 1998, those columns were gathered in *Cocktail: The Drinks Bible for the 21st Century*, a collaboration with *Wired* editor Laura Moorhead.

CONTINUED >

JASMINE, CONTINUED

Cocktail did indeed become one of the early bibles of the mixology movement for dozens of striving bartenders thirsting for knowledge, including Tony Abou-Ganim. Abou-Ganim was one of the reigning bartenders of the San Francisco scene, where he presided over the swanky Starlight Room. When he moved to Las Vegas to become the beverage director at the Bellagio Hotel and Casino, he took the book with him, buying fifty copies for his staff. The drink became the signature cocktail for the Bellagio's high-end Chinese restaurant, also named Jasmine.

As for the man the cocktail is named after, all this history passed by unnoticed. After that first Jasmine cocktail at Townhouse, Matt Jasmin never drank another. He never made the drink at home and never asked for it at bars. When, in 2021, this reporter contacted him about the subject, he was surprised.

"I guess I still don't appreciate it as much as I should," said Jasmin. "I think I'll start asking for it the next time I am out."

1½ ounces gin
¾ ounce lemon juice
¼ ounce Cointreau
¼ ounce Campari
Lemon twist for garnish

Combine all ingredients except the garnish in a cocktail shaker half-filled with ice. Shake until chilled, about 15 seconds. Strain into a chilled cocktail glass. Garnish with the lemon twist.

JULIET & ROMEO

When Toby Maloney opened The Violet Hour, one of the first serious craft cocktail bars to open in the no-nonsense city of Chicago, in 2007, he wanted to create a gin cocktail that would appeal to gin haters. The result was the Juliet & Romeo, a mix of gin, lime juice, cucumber, sugar, mint, salt, and rose water.

"I wanted it to taste like a walk through an English garden," said Maloney. His plan succeeded. The drink has been among the top two sellers for more than a decade. The bar sells an average of twenty per day. Only the Old-Fashioned sells more.

"It's as close to a house drink as we have," said Maloney. It's also jumped to other bars in town. The day of the year when Maloney sees it on the most menus? Valentine's Day, of course.

2 ounces Beefeater gin

¾ ounce lime juice

¾ ounce simple syrup

1 mint sprig

3 cucumber slices

1 tiny pinch salt

1 drop rose water for garnish

3 drops Angostura bitters for garnish

Mint leaf for garnish

Muddle the cucumber slices and salt at the bottom of a cocktail shaker. Add the gin, lime juice, simple syrup, and mint. Fill the shaker halfway with ice. Shake until chilled, about 15 seconds. Strain into a chilled coupe. Garnish with the rose water, bitters, and mint leaf.

KENTUCKY BUCK

While combing through pre-Prohibition cocktail books, San Francisco bartender Erick Castro noticed a dearth of drinks that called specifically for bourbon rather than rye. So he decided to address that issue. He perfected what became the Kentucky Buck while working at the bar Heaven's Dog and the elite speakeasy Bourbon & Branch. The drink debuted at the latter and sold well enough, but it didn't achieve mass appeal until Castro began serving it at the more populist-leaning, high-volume bar Rickhouse. Soon after, bartenders began complaining to Castro because customers asked for the drink at *their* bars. By 2015, it had been adopted by chain restaurants, including some of Guy Fieri's venues. Castro thinks the drink's stubborn adaptability has led to its ubiquity.

"I have seen places online just squeeze a lemon and float strawberry liqueur over a ginger and bourbon, and it all still works," he said.

2 ounces bourbon
1 ripe strawberry
¾ ounce lemon juice
½ ounce simple syrup
2 dashes Angostura bitters
1 ounce ginger beer
Strawberry slice for garnish
Lemon wheel for garnish

Muddle the strawberry, lemon juice, and simple syrup at the bottom of a cocktail shaker. Add the bourbon and bitters. Fill the shaker halfway with ice. Shake until chilled, about 15 seconds. Double strain into a collins glass filled with ice. Top with ginger beer. Garnish with the strawberry slice and lemon wheel.

KILL-DEVIL

There are a lot of candidates in this book for strangest modern classic. Gunshop Fizz, Hard Start, and Death Flip are all in the running. But this unlikely Pegu Club creation by bartender Erin Williams might take the cake. A ragtag collection of aughts-era mixologist obsessions (Rhum agricole! Chartreuse! Overproof rum!), it is crowned by an upturned lime-disc "lily pad" garnish that is filled with the rum and lit on fire. This flamboyant final touch makes the rum drink a cross between an haute craft cocktail and a hokey mid-century tiki stunt drink. According to Williams, who is no longer a bartender, this garnish is not sheerly for looks; the caramelized essential oils add to the flavor and, more importantly, the aroma of the cocktail.

2 ounces La Favorite
rhum agricole blanc

½ ounce green Chartreuse

¼ ounce rich Demerara syrup
(3:1)

3 dashes Angostura bitters

1 lime

5 drops Wray & Nephew
overproof rum

Slice off a disc of lime peel about the size of a poker chip. Remove the white pith by hand and dry with a clean napkin or towel. Invert the lime disc so the rind side is facedown, then shape the inside of the disc into a shallow cup. Set aside.

Combine the rhum, Chartreuse, syrup, and bitters in a mixing glass half-filled with ice and stir until chilled, about 45 seconds. Strain into a chilled coupe. Place the lime disc, pith side up, on a barspoon and very carefully lower it onto the surface of the cocktail. Use an eyedropper to place the 5 drops of overproof rum in the lime disc. Light the overproof rum with a match (never use a lighter). Allow the flame to go out before taking your first sip.

KINGSTON NEGRONI

Back in 2009, during the apex of the cocktail revival, sometimes all it took was the arrival of a new product to spark the creation of a new classic cocktail.

One day in late fall of that year, liquor importer Eric Seed, a Minnesota Johnny Appleseed whose bags were full of not seeds but rare elixirs, walked into the dark, low-ceilinged cavern known as Death & Co. The East Village cocktail bar had been open for only two years or so but was the epicenter of cocktail creativity in New York. It was therefore one of the first stops Seed made whenever he was in town with a new bottle of liquid magic.

On this occasion, the specimen was Smith & Cross, a navy-strength Jamaican-style rum. Standing behind the bar was Phil Ward, Death & Co.'s taciturn head bartender, and Joaquín Simó, Ward's more approachable junior colleague. Both had been on the staff since opening day. The reaction was positive. "I remember comments of 'Hey, it's got the hogo!'" recalled Seed, using the rum term meant to evoke a certain hard-to-define gamey funkiness.

Simó did not wait to discover the rum's mixability potential. He immediately grabbed the bottle and began to build a rum Negroni on the spot—a straightforward application of Ward's "Mr. Potato Head" school of mixology, in which one ingredient in a classic cocktail recipe is replaced with something broadly similar in character.

Simó was not a fan of the then-popular Italian vermouth Carpano Antica. He found it to be a bully that aggressively dominated drinks. But in this case, it made sense. "Smith & Cross is no shrinking violet, so it stands up to the bombastic chocolate and bitter orange notes in the vermouth while drying out the Campari's richness and tempering its bitterness," he explained.

The Kingston Negroni went on the Death & Co. menu in spring of 2010. Simó recalls the cocktail being a hit right away, going over big with its hardcore clientele, then thirsty for anything new in the "brown, boozy, and stirred" category.

That said, the drink was a bit of a sleeper, one that has really come into its own only in the last two or three years. There are several arguable reasons for the increase in popularity, among them the recent flowering of rum and tiki culture and the rise of home bartending (the three-ingredient, equal-parts Kingston Negroni is very easy to make). But perhaps no trend lifted the cocktail's reputation more than the popularity of the original Negroni, which has exploded in the last several years.

Simó is still not sure what possessed him that fateful day in 2009 when—faced with a spirit that he described as redolent of grilled banana bread and smoking allspice branches—he suddenly thought: *aperitivo!*

"It's certainly not the most imaginative thing I've ever done," he admitted, "but it still strikes me as strange."

1 ounce Smith & Cross rum

1 ounce Carpano Antica vermouth

1 ounce Campari

Orange twist for garnish

Combine all ingredients except the garnish in a mixing glass half-filled with ice. Stir until chilled, about 15 seconds. Strain into a double rocks glass over ice. Garnish with the orange twist.

LA PERLA

When bartenders have downtime behind the stick—and they always do—they tend to examine the bottles on the backbar and think thoughts. That's what happened to Jacques Bezuidenhout in 2004 while working at Peche, a Venetian small-plates restaurant in San Francisco. There was a bottle of manzanilla sherry sitting on the shelf that nobody ordered. He mixed it with the Gran Centenario reposado tequila he had been enjoying lately. The result was bone dry, so some sweetness was needed. He thought perhaps the Belle de Brillet pear liqueur being used in another drink on the menu could do the trick. It did.

He named the drink after a tequila-focused restaurant in London run by tequila expert Tomas Estes. Then he entered it in a local sherry cocktail competition and won. At Bezuidenhout's next job, the Mexican restaurant Tres Agaves, La Perla made its first menu appearance. Over time, as the reputations of tequila and sherry rose in cocktail circles, bartenders took up the drink as a superlative example of what could be accomplished with the two formerly unsung mixing ingredients.

1½ ounces reposado tequila
1½ ounces manzanilla sherry
¾ ounce pear liqueur
Lemon twist for garnish

Combine all ingredients except the garnish in a mixing glass half-filled with ice. Stir until chilled, about 15 seconds. Strain into a chilled cocktail glass. Garnish with the lemon twist.

LITTLE ITALY

Audrey Saunders had already racked up a number of modern classics—the Gin-Gin Mule, Earl Grey MarTEAni, and others—by the time she opened Pegu Club in 2005. But she did reserve a couple of soon-to-be classics for the new bar.

One was the Little Italy, which debuted the year the bar opened and which Saunders thinks of as the bar's house Manhattan. It's a simple, three-ingredient cocktail, made of rye, sweet vermouth, and the Italian liqueur Cynar. Everything about the cocktail spoke to the mixology passions of the moment. Manhattan riffs were rampant—the Red Hook (page 124) and Greenpoint (page 77), to name two—and rye was newly ascendant at the time. Amari, too, were being rediscovered.

The idea of adding an amaro instead of bitters to a Manhattan occurred to her during a dinner at the New York restaurant Raoul's. "We were drinking Manhattans right then, and I wondered what one would be like if I substituted Cynar for the Angostura bitters," she said. "Rittenhouse tied it together."

---

2 ounces Rittenhouse bonded rye

¾ ounce Martini & Rossi red vermouth

½ ounce Cynar

Brandied cherry for garnish

Combine all ingredients except the garnish in a mixing glass half-filled with ice. Stir until chilled, about 15 seconds. Strain into a chilled coupe. Garnish with the cherry.

MAXIMILIAN AFFAIR

Boston-based Misty Kalkofen was one of the first modern bartenders to embrace and work with mezcal, a heritage Mexican spirit that has only recently been embraced by drinkers outside of its native Mexico. Prior to 2008, very few mixologists were using the spirit as a cocktail base. Kalkofen, then working at Green Street in Boston, found inspiration in the unexpected appearance of Ron Cooper, the founder of Del Maguey, a line of artisanal, village-specific mezcals. Though she came up with it on the spot, it has become Kalkofen's best-known cocktail.

1 ounce mezcal

1 ounce St-Germain elderflower liqueur

½ ounce Punt e Mes

¼ ounce lemon juice

Lemon twist for garnish

Combine all ingredients except the garnish in a cocktail shaker half-filled with ice. Shake until chilled, about 15 seconds. Strain into a chilled coupe. Express the lemon twist over the surface and drop it into the drink.

MEZCAL MULE

The current boom in mezcal cocktails can arguably be traced back to a few blocks in the East Village neighborhood of New York. There, in 2007 at Death & Co., Phil Ward created the Oaxaca Old-Fashioned. One year later, Jim Meehan, partly inspired by the Oaxaca Old-Fashioned, came up with the Mezcal Mule at PDT.

"I was intrigued with how spirits—peated whisky and mezcal—could be used to impart a smoky quality to cocktails," said Meehan. "There's an old maxim in the wine world that 'if it grows with it, it goes with it.' I brought this concept into the development process. Passion fruit is common in Mexico and has a heady aroma reminiscent of many mezcals' natural, open-vat fermentation. Cucumber, also common, reinforces the vegetal character of the spirit, while the lime and ginger add acidity and earthiness, respectively. A pinch of Mexican chili, which is commonly added to the slices of jicama and oranges served as snacks in mezcalerias, adds heat and more earth."

Like the Oaxaca Old-Fashioned, the influence of the Mezcal Mule can be seen not only in the number of times it has appeared on cocktail menus but also in the number of imitators it bred. There are a lot of Mezcal Mules out there—spurred on by the increased fan base for both mezcal and Moscow Mules—but they don't always go by that name.

1½ ounces mezcal, preferably
Del Maguey Vida
1 ounce Ginger Wort
(recipe follows)
¾ ounce lime juice
¾ ounce Boiron
passion fruit puree
½ ounce agave syrup (1:1)
4 cucumber slices
Candied ginger for garnish
Ground chili for garnish

Muddle 3 of the cucumber slices and the agave syrup in the bottom of a mixing glass, then add the remaining liquid ingredients. Shake with ice, then fine strain into a chilled double old-fashioned glass filled with ice. Garnish with a piece of candied ginger and the remaining slice of cucumber speared together with a cocktail pick and sprinkle with a pinch of ground chili (a salt shaker works well for this).

GINGER WORT
MAKES 25 OUNCES

3 cups (24 ounces) water
1 cup (8 ounces) minced
fresh ginger
1½ ounces light brown sugar
¾ ounce lime juice

Boil the water, then add it to the minced ginger and brown sugar in a nonreactive container. Cover for 90 minutes, then strain through a chinois, pressing the ginger to extract as much liquid as possible. Add the lime juice, bottle, and refrigerate.

MEZCAL MULE

MR. BROWN

Franky Marshall was working at Clover Club in Brooklyn when she came up with this drink in early 2011. It first appeared on their spring menu that year and has since made several more appearances. It is a luxurious, silky, and strong nightcap. It is very similar to a Revolver (page 127) on the rocks, but more complex.

2 ounces bourbon
¾ ounce coffee liqueur
1 dash orange bitters
1 dash Angostura bitters
1 barspoon Vanilla Syrup
(recipe follows)
Orange twist for garnish

Combine all ingredients except the garnish in a mixing glass half-filled with ice. Stir until chilled. Strain into a double rocks glass over one large ice cube. Express the orange twist over the drink, then drop it in.

VANILLA SYRUP

8 ounces sugar
8 ounces water
1 vanilla bean

Combine the sugar and water in a small saucepan. Slice the vanilla bean down the center, scraping out the insides, and add everything directly to the sugar-water mixture. Stir over medium-high heat until it comes to a boil and the sugar has dissolved completely. Remove from the heat and let cool. Taste. If the desired flavor is reached, remove the vanilla bean. If a stronger flavor is needed, leave the solids in the syrup. Pour into a container, cover, and refrigerate. Keeps for 2 weeks.

NAKED AND FAMOUS

Bartender Joaquín Simó was already tinkering with a variation on the Last Word cocktail when he first sampled a Paper Plane (page 113) at Milk & Honey. The Sam Ross creation featured equal parts bourbon, Aperol, lemon juice, and Amaro Nonino, and was itself a riff on the Last Word.

"Trying the Paper Plane for the first time made me rethink the possible candidates for a maraschino liqueur substitute, as I had been stuck in an initial rut of single-flavor liqueurs—curaçao, gentian, et cetera," Simó explained. "I turned my attention to more complex liqueurs like Aperol, Campari, Pimm's, Cynar, and Montenegro. The Aperol–yellow Chartreuse marriage was a big hit, and from there, it was just finding the right mezcal."

The Naked and Famous, which debuted in 2011, has done well by its mentor drink. It is by far the most famous variation on the Paper Plane.

If you can, please use Del Maguey Chichicapa mezcal in this cocktail. It is the original mezcal used in the recipe. Though on the expensive side, it makes a big difference in the taste of the drink.

¾ ounce mezcal
¾ ounce Aperol
¾ ounce yellow Chartreuse
¾ ounce lime juice

Combine the ingredients in a cocktail shaker half-filled with ice. Shake until chilled, about 15 seconds. Strain into a chilled coupe.

OAXACA OLD-FASHIONED

The peak of New York's cocktail revival. A first-time bar owner with everything (and nothing) to lose. A newly minted head bartender at the height of his creativity. An unfamiliar and underutilized spirit. Put those things together, and something wonderful was bound to happen.

The bar was Death & Co. in Manhattan in 2007; the owner, David Kaplan; the bartender, Phil Ward; the spirit, mezcal—at the time little used or understood in bartending circles. The something wonderful? The Oaxaca Old-Fashioned, a simple tequila and mezcal twist on the classic cocktail, introducing hordes of bartenders and drinkers to the versatility of agave spirits.

The drink—composed of reposado tequila, mezcal, two dashes of Angostura bitters, and a barspoon of the then-novel agave syrup, garnished with a flamed orange twist—would go on to be served and imitated the world over, leading to a wave of adventurous new cocktails made with tequila and mezcal—spirits that rarely ventured beyond shots and Margaritas. A dozen years after the cocktail's creation, Death & Co. cemented its status by putting the Oaxaca Old-Fashioned on a T-shirt.

Ward, like most New York bartenders, was new to mezcal at the time. The Oaxaca Old-Fashioned was only the third cocktail in which he used it, the first being a simple Daiquiri with a quarter ounce of mezcal thrown in. The second was a drink called the Cinder, another Daiquiri twist, this one fueled by reposado tequila, jalapeño-infused blanco tequila, and mezcal.

Ward doesn't remember whom he made the first Oaxaca Old-Fashioned for, but he recalls the drink as a "right-off-the-cuff humdinger. The Oaxaca was invented in my favorite time of Death & Co.," Ward recalled. "I feel like it was one big cocktail lab with a slew of guinea pigs—regulars—who would anxiously await the new works in progress every visit."

The cocktail was an immediate favorite. It benefited from not just the novelty of its split spirit base, but also the then-soaring fortunes of the Old-Fashioned. The long-dormant classic cocktail was just beginning to experience a new popularity. For many customers, the comforting format of the straightforward Old-Fashioned acted as a Trojan horse for the untried pleasures of mezcal.

CONTINUED >

OAXACA OLD-FASHIONED, CONTINUED

The flamed orange twist, an eye-catching "ta-da!" that completed the cocktail, undoubtedly boosted the drink's popularity. "Everyone loves pyrotechnics, and I think flamed orange twists get people's eye," said bartender Ivy Mix. "It's called the fajita effect!"

In its earliest rendition, the cocktail was made with El Tesoro reposado tequila and Los Amantes Joven mezcal—ingredients that today are too expensive for most bar programs. But with each new swapped-in tequila or mezcal, the Oaxaca Old-Fashioned demonstrated its endurance.

For Death & Co. owner David Kaplan, the Oaxaca Old-Fashioned was a fait accompli, a cocktail that was destined to be.

"It was a drink that needed to be made," he said, "that probably should have existed already."

1½ ounces reposado tequila, preferably El Tesoro

½ ounce mezcal, preferably Del Maguey San Luis Del Rio

2 dashes Angostura bitters

1 barspoon agave nectar

Flamed orange twist for garnish

Combine all ingredients except the garnish in a rocks glass filled with one large piece of ice. Stir until chilled, about 15 seconds.

To make the flamed orange twist, cut a piece of orange zest about the size of a silver dollar. Hold the piece, skin side down, several inches above the drink. Light a match and use it to warm the skin side of the peel. Quickly squeeze the twist toward the match. The oil from the twist will briefly burst into flame, showering its essence over the drink's surface. Garnish with the twist.

OLD CUBAN

Audrey Saunders envisioned "a Mojito in a little black dress."

"My goal with the Old Cuban was to create a lively yet elegant Champagne cocktail with a neotropical edge," she said. "I wanted to keep the recipe simple and straightforward, something with a sharp, clean yet tangy profile that also provides complexity and effervescence."

The drink—a swanky upgrade on the populist Mojito, using aged rum and Angostura bitters and topping the result with two ounces of Champagne—had been developed by Saunders at the bars Beacon and Tonic. It had its coming-out party at Bemelmans Bar, the 1940s lounge inside the Carlyle. A Champagne drink seemed a natural choice for the timeless, low-lit space, which brims with Old World style and charm.

Saunders read her audience correctly. "After its launch, the Old Cuban took off almost immediately, like a horse out of the gate," she recalled.

The Old Cuban might have remained a local favorite had it not been for the Carlyle's relationship with the Ritz London. The two hotels, which shared a similar moneyed, stylish clientele, often took part in co-promotions. In 2002, the Carlyle sent Saunders to London to do a Bemelmans pop-up at the Ritz. She brought the Old Cuban with her, introducing the drink to a whole new continent. Soon after, the cocktail started landing on menus in London, Paris, and Berlin.

She recalled write-ups mentioning the cocktail in numerous British and European publications, including the *Financial Times* and the *Independent*, among others. "This early period of international press coverage during those trips played a large role in helping the Old Cuban make its way around the world," says Sanders.

1½ ounces aged rum, preferably Bacardi 8 Year Reserva rum

1 ounce simple syrup

¾ ounce lime juice

2 dashes Angostura bitters

6 whole mint leaves

2 ounces Champagne

Muddle the mint leaves, simple syrup, and lime juice at the bottom of a cocktail shaker. Add the rum and bitters. Half-fill the shaker with ice. Shake until chilled, about 15 seconds. Strain into a chilled cocktail glass. Top with the Champagne.

PAPER PLANE

In 2008, Toby Maloney, who helped open The Violet Hour in Chicago, asked bartender Sam Ross, with whom he had worked at Milk & Honey in New York, to create an original cocktail for the bar. Ross came up with a drink he called the Paper Plane, after a song by M.I.A. (The tune's name is actually "Paper Planes.")

The drink first served at The Violet Hour contained Campari. That Italian aperitivo was original to the drink that Ross conceived as an equal-parts riff on the Last Word, the pre-Prohibition cocktail that was resurrected in the aughts by Seattle bartender Murray Stenson. Ross combined the Campari with lemon juice as the citrus element, bourbon as the spirit, and Amaro Nonino, which Ross had recently discovered, as the herbal part of the equation. But two days later, he was having second thoughts.

"I tried it again, and the drink wasn't quite balanced," Ross remembered. "It was slightly too bitter, and the sweetness wasn't there." He subbed in Aperol for the Campari and was immediately satisfied with the result.

Thus was born the bright orange drink that has gone on to conquer the world while inspiring riffs of its own, a shirt, and even a bar's name.

That the Paper Plane took flight was predictable; Ross created it with that purpose. He wanted to invent a drink that was not only balanced and delicious but straightforward, too, relying on four readily available ingredients and requiring no special syrups or infusions. In other words, a cocktail that could be whipped up at any spot with a decent backbar or even at home. The drink doesn't even have a garnish.

Today, the Paper Plane has reached such a level of fame that, thirteen years after its creation, it has begun to raise the question: Is it now *more* popular than Ross's other modern classic cocktail, the Penicillin?

"I still think the Penicillin is more popular, but I'm actually prouder of the Paper Plane because of its simplicity, deliciousness, and its uniqueness," said Ross. "I had never had anything that tasted like that before."

¾ ounce bourbon
¾ ounce Amaro Nonino
¾ ounce Aperol
¾ ounce lemon juice

Combine the ingredients in a cocktail shaker half-filled with ice. Shake until chilled, about 15 seconds. Strain into a chilled coupe.

PENICILLIN

If you ask even a casual cocktail drinker to name an iconic drink of recent vintage, chances are high they will name this creation by Sam Ross, who—alongside Audrey Saunders, Phil Ward, and Dick Bradsell—tops the list of prolific producers of modern classic cocktails. It was partly inspired by the Gold Rush (page 73), another honeyed Whiskey Sour spin also invented at Milk & Honey. The delivery of a shipment of products from Compass Box—an iconoclastic Scotland company that spends its time smashing various suppositions about how scotch should be made and used—led him to spin on the drink. Out went the bourbon, in went blended scotch; the bar's house honey syrup and ginger juice were combined into one syrup; and the whole was topped with a float of smoky Islay scotch. A garnish of candied ginger added a bit of flourish. The name was just common sense. Everything about the recipe—whiskey, lemon, honey, ginger—evoked centuries-old home remedies.

The drink first caught fire at Little Branch, Milk & Honey's sister bar in Greenwich Village. Then Ross brought it to the West Coast when he did some consultancy work in Los Angeles.

The Penicillin has shown great versatility over the years. There have been dozens of takes on the cocktail in bars around the world. Ross is not above stealing from himself. He served a frozen version at his Brooklyn bar Diamond Reef, called the Penichillin, and a hot version during the Covid-19 pandemic, when outdoor dining was the only option at Attaboy.

2 ounces blended scotch

¾ lemon juice

¾ ounce Ginger Honey Syrup (recipe follows)

¼ ounce Islay single malt scotch, preferably Laphroaig 10-year

Candied ginger for garnish

Combine the blended scotch, lemon juice, and syrup in a cocktail shaker half-filled with ice. Shake until chilled, about 15 seconds. Strain into a rocks glass filled with one large cube. Float the Islay scotch on the surface of the drink. Garnish with candied ginger.

GINGER HONEY SYRUP

1 cup honey
6-inch knob of fresh ginger, peeled and sliced
1 cup water

In a small pot, combine the honey, ginger, and water and bring to a boil. Reduce the heat and simmer for 5 minutes. Refrigerate overnight, then strain, discarding the solids.

PIÑA VERDE

Some modern cocktails jump to classic-cocktail status right out of the gate. Other cocktails take their time yet end up in the same rarefied territory.

The Piña Verde, a boozy, herbal twist on the Piña Colada, is one such dark horse. San Diego bartender Erick Castro admits it took years for the simple, four-ingredient drink—green Chartreuse, pineapple juice, lime juice, and coconut cream—to come together. And then it took a few additional years to catch on. All told, the drink's climb to popularity lasted nearly a decade.

It all began with a little bartender trick, designed to make a good drink better—or, at least, stronger.

"I first started with the move of floating green Chartreuse over Piña Coladas," said Castro, recalling a technique he employed in the late aughts. When he became a brand ambassador for Beefeater Gin in 2010, Castro experimented with switching out the traditional rum in the drink for gin. In time, Castro came to realize that what he liked most about the cocktail was the interplay between the Chartreuse and coconut. So he ditched the gin altogether and allowed the overproof French herbal liqueur to step into the starring role.

Castro put the drink on the menu at Polite Provisions, the cocktail bar he cofounded in San Diego in 2012, sometime during the bar's first year of operation. It was then that the drink finally got a proper name. Still, the drink didn't really take off until its debut on the opposite coast, on the opening menu at New York's Boilermaker. The drink first gained traction with industry types. To them, esoteric and challenging heritage products—such as Chartreuse—were culinary catnip and all but guaranteed an order. Local bartenders would sidle up to the bar and ask for "that green Chartreuse drink" they had heard about. Once guests found out what all the bartenders were ordering, they wanted it, too. The profile of the drink received an additional boost from the tiki revival, which was in full flower by 2015 and 2016.

"It is one of those recipes that can bridge the divide between speakeasy and tiki bar," said Castro. It also bridged the divide between high and low drinking, the challenging green liqueur getting along surprisingly well with a traditionally easygoing cocktail.

CONTINUED >

PIÑA VERDE, CONTINUED

1½ ounces green Chartreuse
1½ ounces pineapple juice
¾ ounce Coco Lopez coconut cream
½ ounce lime juice
Pineapple frond for garnish
Lime wheel for garnish

Combine all ingredients except the garnishes in a cocktail shaker half-filled with ice. Shake until chilled, about 15 seconds. Strain into a hurricane glass filled with crushed or pebble ice. Garnish with the pineapple frond and lime wheel.

PORN STAR MARTINI

That a drink called the Porn Star Martini found immediate popularity in the early aughts is shocking to no one. When bartender Douglas Ankrah came up with the decadent mixture of passion fruit puree, passion fruit liqueur, vanilla-flavored vodka (originally Cariel), vanilla syrup, and Prosecco, the inviting flavors paired with the ribald handle made it a must-have at his popular London bars.

However, what *is* unexpected is that its popularity would endure for nearly two decades, to the point that in 2019 it was reported to be the most-ordered cocktail in the United Kingdom.

To most observers, the appeal of the drink boils down to three things: the lurid name, which almost dares you to order the cocktail; the widely popular components; and the novel presentation. The bubbly is not poured atop the drink, in the form of a royale, but comes in a Sidecar as a chaser.

Though widely known as the Porn Star Martini, the drink travels under another name, too: the Maverick Martini, after the Mavericks Gentlemen's Club, a multilevel strip club in Cape Town, South Africa. In 2002, Ankrah was in Cape Town working on his cocktail book, *Shaken and Stirred*, and preparing to open a new London bar called Townhouse. He spent his off-hours at the club. It was on this same trip that the cocktail was conceived. According to Ankrah, the drink simply came to him while walking to work one warm summer morning. "Truly, it was a spur of the moment thing," he said. When Ankrah (who died in August 2021) returned to London, he rechristened it with its second, better-known name.

The cocktail was popular from day one. The bartenders at Townhouse and LAB, which were owned by the same people, couldn't shake them up fast enough. At the time, a new cocktail could not hope for a better launching pad than the two bars, which were not only trendy but also trendsetting.

In recent years, the racy name of the cocktail has proven more of a liability than an asset. In 2019, the British supermarket chain Marks & Spencer was compelled to change the name of a canned version of the drink to the toned-down Passion Star Martini.

Ankrah, for one, was not surprised that his heady creation from the tail end of the "Cool Britannia" days is still showing legs. "The drink is the ultimate party starter," he said in 2020, "sexy, fun, and unpretentious."

CONTINUED >

PORN STAR MARTINI, CONTINUED

1⅓ ounces vanilla-flavored vodka

1⅔ ounces passion fruit puree

½ ounce passion fruit liqueur, preferably Passoã

2 barspoons Vanilla Syrup (page 102)

1 ounce Prosecco

Combine all ingredients except the Prosecco in a cocktail shaker half-filled with ice. Shake until chilled, about 15 seconds. Strain into a chilled cocktail glass. Serve with a shot of Prosecco on the side. (Subsequent renditions of the drink include fresh lime juice, but this recipe is the original.)

RED HOOK

For all of the twentieth century, if you liked Manhattan cocktails, you could order a Manhattan cocktail. But if you felt like something similar, just a bit different, your choices were limited. There was the Perfect Manhattan, with equal parts sweet and dry vermouth, or a Rob Roy, the scotch version of the cocktail.

By the late aughts, however, that all changed. Options for Manhattan-like cocktails increased exponentially. You could order a Little Italy (page 95), made of rye, sweet vermouth, and Cynar; or a Greenpoint (page 77), made of rye, sweet vermouth, yellow Chartreuse, and bitters. There were also the Carroll Gardens, Bushwick, Sunset Park, Bensonhurst, Brooklyn Heights, and the Slope (page 133)—all named after Brooklyn neighborhoods and all containing rye whiskey, vermouth, and usually something bitter.

That trend all began with the Red Hook cocktail, a hybrid of a Manhattan and a Brooklyn created by Italian bartender Vincenzo Errico at Milk & Honey in 2003. As it was composed of rye, maraschino liqueur, and Punt e Mes—three ingredients that were then still relatively obscure but with a slowly growing reputation in the States—bartenders were immediately drawn to the new cocktail. The drink was one-stop shopping for bartenders hoping to turn their customers on to new flavors. Soon afterward, the flood of Manhattan/Brooklyn riffs began.

That almost all of the spin-off drinks had a rye base—as opposed to bourbon, a more common spirit in Manhattans—was no mistake. The Red Hook and its offspring came of age during the rebirth of rye whiskey. Neglected and forgotten for decades, the spicy whiskey found a new home in craft cocktail bars.

After 2010, the storm of rye Manhattan riffs died down. But evidence of that era still lingers. Almost twenty years later, the Red Hook remains a common order, arguably the best-known cocktail to be invented by an Italian bartender since the Negroni. And like the Negroni, it remains more popular in the United States than in Italy—where Errico has since returned to open a bar on the island of Ischia.

---

2 ounces rye
½ ounce maraschino liqueur
½ ounce Punt e Mes

Combine the ingredients in a mixing glass half-filled with ice. Stir until chilled, about 15 seconds. Strain into a chilled coupe.

REVOLVER

A drink named after a gun. A bourbon called Bulleit. A garnish set on fire.

With such sensational elements, perhaps it was preordained that the Revolver, a Manhattan variation created by San Francisco bartender Jon Santer in 2004, should attract attention. But it wasn't as simple as that. There would be a number of serendipitous steps between the drink's creation and its subsequent fame.

Though it clocks in at just four ingredients, including the garnish—bourbon, coffee liqueur, orange bitters, and a flamed orange twist—each element was discerningly selected by Santer, who intentionally created a minimal build.

One of the crucial ingredients in Santer's Revolver was inspired by a friend who always added crème de cacao to his Manhattans. That idea stuck with Santer, whose thoughts eventually turned from chocolate to coffee as a flavoring. At the time, there weren't many coffee liqueurs on the market. Of the few, Santer preferred the rum-based Tia Maria.

As for the bourbon in his coffee-laced Manhattan project, the decision was made for Santer; at Bruno's, the jazz club in San Francisco's Mission District where Santer worked as bar manager, his boss did the liquor buying. One week, he found himself with a case of Bulleit bourbon, a new whiskey no one was going to call for, because no one knew what it was.

To bring the bourbon and Tia Maria together, Santer turned to orange bitters. At the time, bartenders were just rediscovering the once-ubiquitous cocktail ingredient, and only one shop in San Francisco carried it: John Walker & Co. Once a month, Santer would ride his motorcycle down there and buy a few bottles for the bar. As for the eye-catching garnish, Santer gives credit to bartender Dale DeGroff, who made it his trademark.

The drink's name, apart from nodding to the bourbon brand, evoked the gunsmoke aroma emitted by the flamed orange twist.

Santer put the Revolver on Bruno's cocktail list, but the drink didn't make much of an impression. Bruno's wasn't that kind of place. There, most of the guests ordered lagers or whiskey and Cokes; they rarely even looked at the cocktail menu. Instead, it became a drink ordered by fellow bartenders.

It wasn't until the opening of Bourbon & Branch in the city's Tenderloin neighborhood in 2006 that the Revolver gained a real foothold. Patterned after the renowned New York bar Milk & Honey, it boosted the city's cocktail game tenfold. Santer was on the opening bar staff, and his Revolver was the only

CONTINUED >

original cocktail on the debut menu not created by bar director Todd Smith. The trouble was that the menu listed sixty-three drinks, and the Revolver was back on page ten.

The cocktail's fortunes shifted when, a half a year after opening, the wildly popular Bourbon & Branch opened the Library, a standing-only, no-reservations space within the same Jones Street address. The Library's menu listed only a few drinks, and the Revolver was one of them. Bartenders were making fifty to seventy-five Revolvers a night. "I remember my Library colleagues complaining about blackened fingertips from flaming so many orange discs," said Santer.

When the Revolver was subsequently adopted by Milk & Honey and all of Sasha Petraske's other associated bars, including Little Branch and Dutch Kills, its bona fides were certified.

Soon Santer was being sent pictures of Revolver appearances on cocktail lists around the world, from Austria to New Zealand. In 2012, he heard from his friend Patrick Brennan that a bar in Oakland had the Revolver on the menu. When Brennan told the bar manager that his pal Santer—who lived nearby— had invented the drink, the manager scoffed. "The bar manager told my friend the Revolver was a classic from a long time ago," said Santer. "Older than dirt."

2 ounces Bulleit bourbon
½ ounce coffee liqueur
2 dashes orange bitters
Flamed orange twist

Combine all ingredients except the garnish in a mixing glass half-filled with ice. Stir until chilled, about 15 seconds. Strain into a chilled coupe. For the flamed orange twist, cut a piece of orange zest about the size of a silver dollar. Hold the piece, skin side down, several inches above the drink. Light a match and use it to warm the skin side. Quickly squeeze the twist toward the match. The oil from the zest will briefly burst into flame, showering its essence over the drink's surface.

SIESTA

Call it beginner's luck.

In 2006, when Katie Stipe was just starting her bartending career at Flatiron Lounge—one of the early hotbeds of modern mixology in New York City—she came up with the Siesta. A spin on the Hemingway Daiquiri, it combined tequila, lime and grapefruit juices, simple syrup, and Campari.

What made the Siesta challenging in 2006 were the two ingredients Stipe substituted for the Hemingway Daiquiri's usual rum and maraschino liqueur—tequila and Campari. The cocktail bartending community was only starting to reevaluate tequila as a liquor worthy of respect; the spirit was rarely encountered by drinkers in any form beyond the Margarita and Tequila Sunrise.

News of the Siesta spread slowly, mainly by word of mouth. Flatiron was a wellspring of mixology talent, and when bartenders left to pilot other bar programs, they took their recipe knowledge with them, organically building the audience of a given drink.

But the Siesta may have found its true megaphone in the form of Speed Rack, the roving cocktail contest founded in 2011 by Lynnette Marrero and Ivy Mix to highlight the talents of female bartenders nationwide, while simultaneously raising money for breast cancer education, prevention, and research. In each round of Speed Rack competition, bartenders are called upon to create several drinks from memory as fast and accurately as possible. Thrown into the mix of possible drinks, beginning in 2015, was Stipe's Siesta. It has since been featured in Speed Rack bouts in the United Kingdom, Canada, and Australia.

Stipe went on from Flatiron to work at more than a dozen bars. The list of original cocktails she has invented is hundreds long. But the Siesta has held its place as her best-known creation.

"It seems like a no-brainer recipe now," Stipe said. "It wasn't then."

1½ ounces tequila
¾ ounce lime juice
¾ ounce simple syrup
½ ounce grapefruit juice
¼ ounce Campari
Lime wheel for garnish

Combine all ingredients except the garnish in a cocktail shaker half-filled with ice. Shake until chilled, about 15 seconds. Strain into a chilled coupe. Garnish with the lime wheel.

SINGLE VILLAGE FIX

The Single Village Fix, an early modern mezcal cocktail, is not just one of San Francisco bar owner Thad Vogler's best-known creations; it's one of his "only creations," said Vogler.

"Like Sasha Petraske, I've been less interested in innovation or invention," explained Vogler. Instead, he'd rather hone his execution of long-established classic cocktails. "Agave spirits are a bit of an exception because they are less represented in the canon."

Mezcals run the gamut in flavor, from vegetal to fruity. The latter style reminded Vogler of pineapple, so in 2008 he paired it with a pineapple gum syrup that he had developed with Jennifer Colliau to use in Pisco Punch. (Colliau went on to found Small Hand Foods, which now commercially produces the syrup.) He put it on the opening menu at Beretta, a pizzeria with a top-shelf cocktail program of his devising. It was a popular order right off.

"Beretta and my home were and are in the Mission, the Spanish-speaking part of the city," said Vogler. "I wanted to represent the spirit in the neighborhood, and it's such a beautiful spirit. Also, I'm interested in provenance with spirits, so the single village mezcals were some of the few spirits that are traceable that way." He later featured it on the menu of his first bar and restaurant, the influential Bar Agricole.

"I feel it's emblematic of my career," he said. "The drink is simple. It's basically a Milk & Honey drink with an eye toward the quality of the spirit and ingredients."

1½ ounces mezcal
¾ ounce Small Hand Foods pineapple gum syrup
¾ ounce lime juice

Combine the ingredients in a cocktail shaker half-filled with ice. Shake until chilled, about 15 seconds. Strain into a chilled coupe.

THE SLOPE

Julie Reiner wanted both a house Martini and house Manhattan on the menu when her Brooklyn bar Clover Club opened in 2009. The result was the Gin Blossom (page 69) and this drink, named after the Brooklyn neighborhood of Park Slope, where she lived then. She got lucky in that both drinks soon were popular with guests. Like many New York bartenders at the time, she was influenced by the Red Hook (page 124), a Brooklyn/Manhattan spin by Milk & Honey bartender Vincenzo Errico.

"I was aware of the drink and really loved it," recalled Reiner. "It influenced me in that I learned from the recipe that the Manhattan could be edited slightly to create new and equally delicious cocktails." Like the Red Hook, the Slope featured the then-trendy Italian spirit Punt e Mes. The drink remains a top seller at Clover Club.

2½ ounces rye

¾ ounce Punt e Mes

¼ ounce apricot liqueur, preferably Rothman & Winter Orchard apricot liqueur

1 dash Angostura bitters

Cherry for garnish

Combine the ingredients in a mixing glass half-filled with ice. Stir until chilled, about 15 seconds. Strain into a chilled cocktail glass and garnish with the cherry.

TIA MIA

TIA MIA

The name of this drink is an anagram for Mai Tai, the classic tiki drink of which this is a mezcal interpretation. Ivy Mix, who co-owns Leyenda, the Brooklyn bar devoted to Latin spirits, invented the drink for Lani Kai, a short-lived tiki bar in Manhattan owned by her mentor, Julie Reiner. When Reiner and Mix opened Leyenda, the Tia Mia went on the menu. It has stayed there ever since and been a dependable seller. The cocktail has since appeared in many cocktail books.

1 ounce Del Maguey Vida mezcal

1 ounce Appleton Estate Reserve Jamaica rum

½ ounce toasted almond orgeat, preferably Orgeat Works t'Orgeat almond syrup

½ ounce curaçao, preferably Pierre Ferrand

¾ ounce lime juice

Lime wheel for garnish

Pineapple frond for garnish

Edible orchid for garnish

Combine all ingredients except the garnishes in a cocktail shaker filled with ice. Shake until chilled, about 15 seconds. Strain into a chilled double old-fashioned glass filled with crushed ice. Garnish with the lime wheel, pineapple frond, and edible orchid.

TOMMY'S MARGARITA

Perhaps more than any other modern classic, Tommy's Margarita came together almost by accident, over the course of a decade. For those hoping to pin down an exact year of origin, abandon all hope. "There is no date," said its creator, Julio Bermejo, whose family owns Tommy's Mexican Restaurant in San Francisco, for which the drink is named. "The style of Margarita made by Tommy's evolved."

The seeds of the drink were planted when Bermejo was not yet of drinking age. Like many teenagers, he experimented with booze. Beer, rum, and brandy left him with bad hangovers. But he found that tequila—filched from Tommy's, his family's restaurant in the Richmond District—didn't do as much damage. And Herradura tequila in particular, made of 100 percent agave, left his brain largely unscathed.

Years later, in the late 1980s, when Bermejo took up his post behind the bar at Tommy's, he drew on that misspent youth and switched out the mixto tequila being used in the house Margarita for Herradura.

"Our pour cost went up dramatically," he recalled, "and the drink's cost went up only like fifty cents." But for Bermejo, the change in flavor made it worth it.

Though the Tommy's Margarita is famous for containing no curaçao—a defining ingredient in a Margarita—eighty-sixing that liqueur was never a decision Julio had to make. Triple sec had once been used in the house Marg, which was of the blended sort common in that era. But by the time Bermejo arrived, it had vanished from the recipe, probably for economic reasons, and been supplanted by simple syrup.

Replacing the simple syrup with agave syrup, however, *was* Bermejo's idea.

"Agave syrup was a product used mainly by California health-food producers," he said. "But even though it was expensive, it was a no-brainer for me. It was a product from a similar plant as tequila." He also traded up from sour mix to freshly squeezed lime juice and discouraged the use of a salted rim, seeing the flourish as unnecessary.

Over the years, Bermejo began favoring Margaritas served on the rocks over the blended variety. By the end of the '90s, Tommy's Margarita orders had gone from being 95 percent blended to 95 percent on the rocks.

For all his innovations, however, Tommy's Mexican Restaurant was still in the Richmond; Bermejo was working in a vacuum. Then one day in 1995 or 1996, Bermejo was discovered by the greater bartending world in the form of Tony Abou-Ganim, one of the most celebrated bartenders in San Francisco. When

CONTINUED >

TOMMY'S MARGARITA, CONTINUED

Abou-Ganim became the beverage director at the Bellagio Hotel and Casino in Las Vegas in 1997, Bermejo was brought on as a consultant. By then, Tommy's was beginning to get regular local press about their tequila selection. In 1999, the *Wall Street Journal* published a long article on tequila and called Tommy's "the epicenter" of the spirit's revival. The piece cemented Bermejo's reputation as a tequila expert.

The very last thing to come into focus about the Tommy's Margarita was the name. And Bermejo had nothing to do with that. He credits two British bartenders, Henry Besant and Dre Masso, with its inadvertent christening.

In 2001, Bermejo traveled to the UK and Europe with the Tequila Regulatory Council (known as the CRT) to aid the organization in getting the spirit officially recognized by the EU. Bermejo's job was to connect to the English-speaking bartenders. In London, he met Dre Masso, who was a bartender at the white-hot LAB bar. The next year, Masso asked permission to visit Bermejo; he spent six months in 2003 listening to Bermejo's stories and tasting tequila.

"It was at this point that I discovered his house cocktail," said Masso. "When you looked around the bar and restaurant, it seemed every guest had a sipping tequila in one hand and a Tommy's in the other."

Masso and Besant (who died in 2013) became the drink's two town criers, telling colleagues about it and talking it up at cocktail demonstrations as founders of the Worldwide Cocktail Club, a consultancy they formed in the mid-aughts. Masso and Besant even opened a Mexican restaurant and tequila bar in London called Green & Red and coauthored *Margarita Rocks* in 2005, which includes what may be the first book mention of the Tommy's Margarita. The name came easy.

"The cocktail was so synonymous with Tommy's restaurant that, in my mind, it has always been called that," said Masso.

2 ounces reposado tequila
1 ounce lime juice
½ ounce agave syrup
Kosher salt for rim
Lime wedge for garnish

Dip half of the rim of a rocks glass in lime juice and then salt. Set aside. Combine all ingredients except the garnish in a cocktail shaker half-filled with ice. Shake until chilled, about 15 seconds. Strain into a prepared rocks glass filled with ice. Garnish with the lime wedge.

TRIDENT

The Trident is an ode to obscurity and the only drink in this book not created by a bartender. Robert Hess of Seattle was a tech executive at Microsoft in the 1990s and an amateur home mixologist. He has a soft spot for obscure cocktail ingredients, including bitters. He had been on the hunt for orange bitters—a critical ingredient in an old-school Martini—for years, and he finally found Fee Brothers, a manufacturer in Rochester, New York. Hess ordered a case of each of the bitters they were then making: orange, mint, "old-fashioned," and peach.

The peach bitters became the first building block of an eventual project to build an "obscured Negroni," as Hess put it. He had already discovered that aquavit made a nifty substitute for gin in the Italian cocktail. Maybe, he surmised, there were other neglected bottles that needed a leg up. For the Campari, he reached for another intense Italian liqueur, the artichoke-informed Cynar. And dry sherry replaced the vermouth. He called the drink the Trident, a nod to the three seafaring countries that produced the trio of liquors.

He tested his invention on the bartenders of the Zig Zag Café, the only Seattle bar that could be counted on to have the three main ingredients on hand. (Hess carried the peach bitters on his person wherever he went.) They liked it; so much so that the next time he dropped in, the Trident was on the cocktail menu. Soon the state Liquor Control Board was asking why Zig Zag was ordering more Cynar than all of the other Seattle bars combined.

The Trident might have remained strictly a local favorite if Brian Miller, a Seattle native and bartender at the recently opened Pegu Club in New York, had not stopped by the Zig Zag for a drink in late 2005. He was so taken with the Trident that he took the recipe back to Gotham and began selling them at Pegu Club. Exposure on Hess's own Drinkboy internet chat room, which became a sort of virtual Mermaid Tavern for the cocktail geek set, also boosted the drink's reputation.

---

1 ounce fino, manzanilla, or amontillado sherry
1 ounce aquavit
1 ounce Cynar
2 dashes peach bitters
Lemon twist for garnish

Combine all ingredients except the garnish in a mixing glass half-filled with ice. Stir until chilled, about 15 seconds. Strain into a chilled coupe. Garnish with the lemon twist.

VODKA ESPRESSO, AKA ESPRESSO MARTINI

She wasn't Kate Moss. She wasn't Naomi Campbell. In fact, the mysterious model—who, according to legend, asked bartender Dick Bradsell one night at the Soho Brasserie in London in the 1980s for a drink that would "fuck me up and then wake me up"—may not have been a model at all.

"He told me he couldn't even remember who it was and he just assumed she was a model," says Miranda Dickson, global brand director at Absolut Elyx, who interviewed Bradsell about the drink in 2011, five years before he died.

But Beatrice Bradsell, the late bartender's daughter, insists there was indeed a model.

"Unfortunately, I don't know the name of the model," said Bradsell. "He took that to the grave. I do know it was a true story, but he loved the mystery that came with the unrevealed identity."

The never-to-be-known woman is just one of many details about the Espresso Martini that have been obscured by the mists of time. Even the very name of the drink is a matter of dispute. It began its long, robust journey through the world's bars under the prosaic moniker Vodka Espresso. Sometime in the late 1990s it evolved into the Espresso Martini, the name that stuck. It also enjoyed a brief, fevered notoriety from 1998 to 2003 as the Pharmaceutical Stimulant.

Along the way, the drink changed as often as its name. The cocktail originally served at the Soho Brasserie on Old Compton Street was an off-menu special Dick Bradsell bestowed on favored friends and colleagues. There was no coffee liqueur in the drink at the time; only, as the name would indicate, shots of vodka and espresso, tied together by a little simple syrup. The mixture was served on the rocks and topped with the now-iconic garnish of three espresso beans.

When exactly Bradsell came up with the potion that would become his calling card is likewise a matter of conjecture. Some sources say 1983, but Beatrice Bradsell thinks otherwise.

"Dad told me they were filming the David Bowie film *Absolute Beginners* in Soho at the time," explained Bradsell. "The film was released in 1986, which makes me think the drink was created in 1985."

CONTINUED >

VODKA ESPRESSO,
AKA ESPRESSO MARTINI, CONTINUED

But it would take another decade or so for the cocktail to become news. The drink didn't appear on a menu until Jonathan Downey hired Bradsell at his bar Match EC1, which opened to acclaim in September 1997.

"I'm certain hardly anyone would have had this drink or heard of it before Match," said Downey. "It was hugely popular and a real revelation."

The cocktail served at Match was a transitional version in the drink's tangled timeline. It still went by the name Vodka Espresso but was made with coffee liqueur in lieu of simple syrup and, critically, was served up in a stemmed glass. According to Beatrice Bradsell, her father had never been completely satisfied with the drink and kept tinkering with it.

"He thought of where he wanted it to sit, and his mind went to dessert-style cocktails and the Brandy Alexander," said Bradsell. "In his mind, the Brandy Alexander works so well because it took two quite different flavors [brandy and cream] and used modifiers to bridge the gaps in the palate. He worked to do the same with his cocktail by using various coffee liqueurs and shaking it to improve the texture."

By the end of the 1990s, these changes had stuck, along with a new name: Espresso Martini.

Most people blame the 'tini craze of the 1990s for forcing a new identity on the Vodka Espresso. "Everything was 'tini-tastic in London," said Dickson. "The Martini was such a movement. That's when the Vodka Espresso grew into the Espresso Martini."

Dick Bradsell wasn't quite done with his invention after Match, though. In 1998, Damien Hirst, the English artist who was briefly besotted with cocktail culture, opened his own bar called Pharmacy in Notting Hill. Bradsell, hired to create the drink program, rechristened his Vodka Espresso/Espresso Martini as the Pharmaceutical Stimulant. It was now back on the rocks.

Anything Dick Bradsell put his hand to at that point was noteworthy, so the drink, whatever its name, spread like wildfire.

As to the drink's unending appeal, Downey points to the obvious—the one-two punch the cocktail embodies. It's popular, he said, "for the reasons Dick has so brilliantly shared—it wakes you up and fucks you up!"

2 ounces vodka
1 ounce fresh-brewed espresso
½ ounce coffee liqueur
¼ ounce simple syrup
3 espresso beans for garnish

Combine all ingredients except the garnish in a cocktail shaker half-filled with ice. Shake until chilled, about 15 seconds. Strain into a chilled coupe. Garnish with the espresso beans.

WHISKEY APPLE HIGHBALL

It isn't plausible to credit just one bartender with inventing such a simple drink. But Shady Pines Saloon in Sydney, and later the Baxter Inn in the same city—both owned by the same team, including Anton Forte and Jason Scott—certainly perfected and popularized this unusual highball.

Shady Pines, a Western-themed bar, has always had a whiskey focus. A short time after opening, the owners began to pair that whiskey with freshly pressed green apple juice, using a Breville juicer. The novel combination was a hit with the public immediately, partly due to the eye-catching vivid green color of the drink. The cocktail never really had a proper name, and it wasn't on the menu. (Forte called it "Whiskey Apple.") People just knew it was available and ordered it.

Soon bars across Sydney were serving the drink. Beginning in 2017, the highball hopped the Pacific and began showing up on menus at New York cocktail bars like Diamond Reef, Suffolk Arms, and Peppi's Cellar (opened by Scott himself). Good-quality Granny Smith apples, freshly pressed, are essential to the success of the drink. The original whiskey used at the beginning was Jim Beam rye, but many other ryes work just as well.

---

1 ounce rye whiskey

4 ounces freshly pressed Granny Smith apple juice

Combine the ingredients in a highball glass filled with ice. Stir briefly.

WHITE NEGRONI

Necessity is the mother of invention. And sometimes a Negroni is an absolute necessity.

Such was the case one hot summer night in 2001 in a small town in Bordeaux. Nick Blacknell, then the director of Plymouth Gin, was traveling from England to France to attend Vinexpo, a spirits exhibition, alongside rising London bartender Wayne Collins, who was there to compete in the Drinks International cocktail competition. The day before the contest, they settled into a guesthouse in Médoc. Soon the relentless heat had Blacknell hankering for a bracing, ice-cold Negroni. With no promising bar options in their village, the duo turned to the local liquor store to rustle up the necessary ingredients: traditionally gin, Campari, and sweet vermouth.

Once in the store, Collins remembered, they were confronted by the usual array of then rather obscure French liqueurs and aperitifs. "I suggested we make the Negronis with French ingredients, as it seemed more appropriate." They settled on Suze and Lillet Blanc. Given that both men were in town on gin business, the base spirit remained constant.

Later that afternoon and several fairer Negronis later, all garnished with a wedge of fresh pink grapefruit—a twist that Collins was known to favor in Martinis, and one that he thought would lend a bittersweet lift to the drink— Blacknell's marketing mind went to work. He suggested that, once back home, they should promote the new drink, christened the White Negroni, in the UK.

The cocktail did not catch on. Despite the efforts of Collins and Blacknell, it was quietly forgotten for many years. Ironically, the White Negroni got its big break not in the drink's birthplace or in England, the home of its inventor, but in the United States—at a time when Suze was still unavailable there. In 2002, Simon Ford was hired by Blacknell as brand ambassador for Plymouth gin and charged with turning the vodka-loving United States back into a nation of gin drinkers. He took the White Negroni and ran with it, introducing it and other gin cocktails to any bar owner who had even a passing interest in the spirit. That included Audrey Saunders, then bar director at New York's Bemelmans Bar in the Hotel Carlyle.

To get around the Suze problem, Saunders smuggled bottles on her many trips to and from England. She did the same at Pegu Club after it opened in 2005

CONTINUED >

and, after stumbling upon a small quantity of Suze online, went one better, putting the drink on the bar's menu.

"Illegal, of course," admitted Saunders, "but from my part it was more about doing whatever was necessary to expand awareness about artisanal products in those early days."

Eventually, demand for Suze among American bartenders grew strong enough that Pernod Ricard began to import the liqueur in 2012. After that, there was no holding back the White Negroni. As the aughts rolled into the 2010s, the drink's popularity only increased, raised by the reborn fortunes of the original Negroni and the public's thirst for any variation—all of which identify Collins as one of the most prescient mixologists of his day.

1 ounce Plymouth gin
1 ounce Lillet Blanc
1 ounce Suze
Grapefruit twist for garnish

Combine all ingredients except the garnish in a mixing glass half-filled with ice. Stir until chilled, about 15 seconds. Strain into a chilled cocktail glass. Garnish with the grapefruit twist.

WIBBLE

Only a handful of modern classic cocktails have been named after living people. This creation by Dick Bradsell, the dean of the London cocktail revival, is one of them.

The honoree is Nick Blacknell, a liquor-world executive who has done much over the years to burnish the reputations of Plymouth gin and Havana Club rum, among other labels. According to Blacknell, Bradsell was working at the London bar The Player at the time. One night Blacknell, fairly drunk and dressed up in a woman's fur coat, confessed he was jealous that Dick had named a drink at Detroit—another London bar Bradwell worked at—after another regular customer. Bradsell responded by whipping up a potion made partly of Plymouth gin and Plymouth sloe gin—logical, given that Blacknell was promoting those brands at the time.

"I remember clearly he made it from scratch in a single go, no practice, no pause for thought," recalled Blacknell. "And we tasted it and it was delicious, with that sweet-sour, yin-yang tanginess and balance from the sloe, mure, and grapefruit."

Blacknell wanted to call it the Nick Martini. Bradsell didn't think that was a very good handle. He suggested the Weeble Martini, named after the toy, as Blacknell always wobbled when he drank, but never fell down. Then he had second thoughts and said, "No, Weeble might sue me. We better call it the Wibble instead."

1 ounce gin
1 ounce sloe gin
1 ounce grapefruit juice
¾ teaspoon lemon juice
¾ teaspoon simple syrup (2:1)
¾ teaspoon crème de mure
Lemon twist for garnish

Combine all ingredients except the garnish in a cocktail shaker half-filled with ice. Shake until chilled, about 15 seconds. Strain into a chilled coupe. Garnish with the lemon twist.

WILDEST REDHEAD

New York bartender Meaghan Dorman created this drink in 2011 while work-ing at Lantern's Keep, a snug cocktail bar at the Iroquois Hotel in midtown Manhattan. Landing somewhere between a Scotch sour and the cocktail Remember the Maine, it is Dorman's most well-traveled drink. Her inspiration was a Cherry Heering and lemon cocktail called the Wild Redhead, found in *Jones' Complete Barguide* (1977) by Stan Jones, one of the few comprehensive cocktail bartending books published during the 1970s.

1½ ounces blended scotch
¾ ounce lemon juice
½ ounce rich honey syrup (3:1)
¼ ounce allspice dram
¼ ounce Cherry Heering

Combine all ingredients except the Cherry Heering in a cocktail shaker half-filled with ice and shake until chilled, about 15 seconds. Strain into a rocks glass filled with one large ice cube. Carefully float the Cherry Heering over the cube.

WINCHESTER

Brian Miller, who cut his teeth at Pegu Club and Death & Co., was New York's fiercest apostle of the tiki revival that took root in the 2000s. Among his innovations was to layer gin the same way rum typically was in many classic tiki drinks. Thus was born this drink during Miller's brief reign, alongside bartender Lynnette Marrero, at the restaurant Elettaria. The cocktail never made the menu there but subsequently landed on the list at Death & Co. It has since become a signature drink for Miller.

When he opened his tiki bar the Polynesian in 2018, he revamped the recipe as the Double-Barreled Winchester, using four gins instead of three. Only the Martin Miller's Westbourne Strength remained constant—perhaps for sentimental reasons, given the gin's name. The original recipe is featured here. (The drink is named for Angus Winchester, a former global ambassador for Tanqueray gin. A fortunate man, Winchester also lent his name to another cult classic cocktail, the Beuser and Angus Special, created by Gonçalo de Sousa Monteiro at the Victoria Bar in Berlin, Germany. For anyone reading this, I am still waiting for someone to name a cocktail after me.)

1 ounce Martin Miller's Westbourne Strength gin
1 ounce Hayman's Old Tom gin
1 ounce Tanqueray gin
¾ ounce lime juice
¾ ounce grapefruit juice
¾ ounce St-Germain elderflower liqueur
½ ounce grenadine
¼ ounce ginger syrup
1 dash Angostura bitters
Lime wheel for garnish
Cherry for garnish

Combine all ingredients except the garnishes in a cocktail shaker half-filled with ice. Shake until chilled, about 15 seconds. Strain into a tiki mug and top with crushed ice. Garnish with a lime wheel skewered with a cherry.

1910

Ezra Star, a leading light in the Boston cocktail scene and the guiding force of the Boston cocktail bar Drink for many years, created this one on the fly for a cocktail competition in 2011. The original had a combination of Del Maguey Tobala mezcal and Louis XIII cognac. You need not go that fancy with the spirits to make the drink work. It will be a deep, dense, and rich cocktail no matter what. The name refers to the year the Mexican Revolution began.

1 ounce Punt e Mes
¾ ounce mezcal
¾ ounce cognac
½ ounce maraschino liqueur
2 dashes Peychaud's bitters
Orange twist for garnish

Combine all ingredients except the garnish in a mixing glass half-filled with ice. Stir until chilled, about 15 seconds. Strain into a chilled coupe. Express the orange twist over the surface, then drop it in.

ACKNOWLEDGMENTS

The work of many people and many years went into the creation of this book. I would first like to thank the following bartenders for their creative and timeless contributions: Tony Abou-Ganim, Tiffanie Barriere, Julio Bermejo, Jeff Berry, Jacques Bezuidenhout, Damon Boelte, Jacob Briars, Salvatore Calabrese, Erick Castro, Toby Cecchini, Stephen Cole, Wayne Collins, Kyle Davidson, Dale DeGroff, Marcovaldo Dionysos, Meaghan Dorman, Vincenzo Errico, Kirk Estopinal, Tonia Guffey, Charles Hardwick, Paul Harrington, Robert Hess, Chris Hysted-Adams, Misty Kalkofen, Nicole Lebedevitch, Don Lee, Greg Lindgren, Michael McIlroy, Toby Maloney, Franky Marshall, Jim Meehan, Joerg Meyer, Brian Miller, Ivy Mix, Jeffrey Morgenthaler, Maksym Pazuniak, Julie Reiner, Sam Ross, Jon Santer, Audrey Saunders, T. J. Siegal, Joaquín Simó, Todd Smith, Ezra Star, Katie Stipe, Thad Vogler, Phil Ward, and Erin Williams, as well as the late Douglas Ankrah and Dick Bradsell.

Many thanks to the talented and tireless staff at Ten Speed Press, including Aaron Wehner, Julie Bennett, Kim Keller, Betsy Stromberg, Annie Marino, Jane Chinn, Chloe Aryeh, Allison Renzulli, and David Hawk. Much gratitude to photographer Lizzie Munro for her reliably excellent work; this is our third collaboration in a row. Thanks to Jeff Bell, Ivy Mix, Pedro Rojas, Javelle Taft, and Haley Traub for their deft preparation and styling of the cocktails at, respectively, PDT, Leyenda, Clover Club, Death & Co., and Attaboy. Additional thanks to the drinks website Punch, where I often had the opportunity to write at length on the subject of modern classic cocktails. I also owe a deep debt of gratitude to Martin Doudoroff, who many years ago suggested we work together on an app about modern classic cocktails. Much of the research and work that went into that app, which was published in 2016, led to this book.

Finally, as always, my undying love to my wife, Mary Kate Murray, whose love and support sustains me as nothing else has in my entire life; and my son, Asher, and stepson, Richard, who make me proud every day.

ABOUT THE AUTHOR & PHOTOGRAPHER

ROBERT SIMONSON writes about bars, bartenders, cocktails, spirits, and travel for the *New York Times*, where he has been a contributor since 2000. He is the author of five books of cocktail history, including *The Old-Fashioned* (2014), which kicked off an ongoing cottage industry of single-drink cocktail books; *A Proper Drink* (2016), the first, and so far only, history of the current cocktail renaissance; *3-Ingredient Cocktails* (2017); *The Martini Cocktail* (2019); and *Mezcal and Tequila Cocktails* (2021). Both *3-Ingredient Cocktails* and *Martini* were nominated for James Beard Awards. He is also the recipient of the 2019 Spirited Award for Best Cocktail and Spirits Writer and 2020 Spirited Award for Best Cocktail Book for *Martini*; and a 2021 IACP Award for narrative beverage writing. He is the co-author, with Martin Doudoroff, of two apps, "Modern Classics of the Cocktail Renaissance" and "The Martini Cocktail." In January 2022, he launched his Substack newsletter "The Mix with Robert Simonson." A native of Wisconsin, he has one son, Asher, a stepson, Richard, and lives in Brooklyn with his wife, Mary Kate Murray.

LIZZIE MUNRO is a photographer, art director, and writer, whose work has spanned the food and drink space. Most recently, her focus has been on cocktails—both photographing them and enjoying them—in her role as art director for the James Beard Award–winning media brand Punch. This book marks her third collaboration with Robert Simonson. A graduate of Bard College, she lives in Brooklyn, New York. When pressed to choose just one, her favorite Modern Classic is the Greenpoint.

INDEX

Hand image on Table of Contents © Suraphol -
stock.adobe.com
Geometric shape pattern © zionbalkon -
stock.adobe.com
Paper texture © nata777_7 - stock.adobe.com
Newspaper image © LiliGraphie - stock.adobe.com

Typefaces: Monotype's Bauer Bodoni Std, Linotype's
Bodoni LT Pro, Colophon Foundry's Central Avenue,
and Klim Type Foundry's Founders Grotesk

Library of Congress Cataloging-in-Publication Data
Names: Simonson, Robert, author. | Munro, Lizzie, author.
Title: Modern classic cocktails : 60+ stories and recipes from the new golden age in drinks / by
    Robert Simonson ; photographs by Lizzie Munro.
Description: First edition. | California : Ten Speed Press, [2022] | Includes index.
Identifiers: LCCN 2021052404 (print) | LCCN 2021052405 (ebook) |
    ISBN 9781984857767 (hardcover) | ISBN 9781984857774 (ebook)
Subjects: LCSH: Cocktails. | Alcoholic beverages. | Cookbooks. lcgft
Classification: LCC TX951 .S583633 2022 (print) | LCC TX951 (ebook) |
    DDC 641.87/4—dc23/eng/20211230
LC record available at https://lccn.loc.gov/2021052404
LC ebook record available at https://lccn.loc.gov/2021052405

Hardcover ISBN: 978-1-9848-5776-7
eBook ISBN: 978-1-9848-5777-4

Printed in China

Acquiring editor: Julie Bennett | Editor: Kim Keller
Designer: Annie Marino | Production designers: Faith Hague and Mari Gill
Production and prepress color manager: Jane Chinn
Contributing photo retoucher: Jeremy Blum
Copyeditor: Kristi Hein | Proofreader: Kathy Brock | Indexer: Ken DellaPenta
Publicist: David Hawk | Marketer: Chloe Aryeh

10 9 8 7 6 5 4 3 2 1

First Edition